WITHDRAWN

# THOREAU IN
# OUR SEASON

To Reginald L. Cook

**HENRY DAVID THOREAU, AET. 44**

# THOREAU IN OUR SEASON

Edited with an
Introduction by
John H. Hicks

THE UNIVERSITY OF
MASSACHUSETTS PRESS

PS
3053
.H5

Copyright © 1962, 1966 by
*The University of Massachusetts Press*

"Thoreau in Italy," copyright © 1962 by
Robert Francis, originally appeared in
*The Massachusetts Review*
Spring 1962

MR

Library of Congress Catalog Card Number 65-26241
Printed in the United States of America

12266

# CONTENTS

# INTRODUCTION

## JOHN H. HICKS

MOST OF THE CONTRIBUTIONS to this collection first appeared in *The Massachusetts Review* for Autumn 1962 under the title of "A Centenary Gathering for Henry David Thoreau." To the original collection have now been added two new essays and a poem.

The one-hundredth anniversary of Thoreau's death in 1962 seemed an occasion to summon extra effort from a journal of literature, the arts and public affairs published in Thoreau's home territory, and which had adopted its name and many of its ideals from the *Massachusetts Quarterly Review* of 1847 edited by Ralph Waldo Emerson and Theodore Parker. Our intention was to mark Thoreau's centennial with a gathering of criticism of and fresh reaction to Thoreau in our time. While vigilant for what we could secure of new scholarship, our wish also was to find contributions beyond the exclusively academic, beyond the specialist writing to other specialists. The result is a combination of essays, poems, memoirs, letters, art and photographs, that cover a wide diversity of tone and subject, and yet penetrate to appreciable depth. Our deepest wish, among others, has been to see Thoreau's relevance in the climate of post-existentialist thought; to show if we could what a Thoreau relevant to our day and predicament looks like. We have sought in a few instances to provide first-hand evidence of Thoreau's significance for persons actually caught up in important or typical contemporary events that have put Thoreauvian values and strategies to new test in our season.

Perhaps much of the merit this gathering possesses—but certainly what differentiates it from other collections on Thoreau presently in print—derives from the degree, albeit limited, to which this purpose has been achieved. Our gathering is the first to have documented the immediacy of Thoreau's relevance for intellectuals and strategists of the Negro revolution in America; and for those—in South Africa, Denmark, America and elsewhere—committed to the cause of civil liberties in the twentieth-century turmoil of war, of the super-state and police state, of vast changes social and political. The predominant (but not exclusive) image of Thoreau that emerges from this volume has its epiphany in the drawing by Leonard Baskin which prefaces the collection, a rendering of haunting force and a Thoreau few critics heretofore have visualized.

The protestation by Martin Luther King which opens this gathering was virtually dictated from the jail house in Albany, Georgia, in the full heat of the resistance in that city in September

INTRODUCTION

1962. The essay by the distinguished Negro philosopher William
Stuart Nelson has for its generating impulse not only a knowledge
of Thoreau but a lifetime of participation with Gandhi in India,
and more than a decade of leading, for students from all over the
world, seminars in the philosophy of non-violent resistance. The
account by Willard Uphaus, a retrospect upon many months of litigation and imprisonment, is record of a confrontation—during the
height of the McCarthy hysteria in America—with state power in
New Hampshire, and with troubled, narrowly-divided opinion
among justices of the Supreme Court in New Hampshire and of
the United States Supreme Court in Washington, D. C.

Other evidence is provided here of Thoreau's relevance tested
under pressure of contemporary history. There is a memorable declaration by the Reverend T. N. W. Bush, formerly of Johannesburg
and associated with the forming of the now banned African National Congress, who against the background of the Sharpville
Shooting writes of Thoreau's significance for himself and individuals like Chief Albert Luthuli in profoundly disturbed South
Africa. A small essay entitled "Thoreau and the Danish Resistance" details the meaning "Civil Disobedience" held for a small
number of Danes who in the face of Nazi brutality in Denmark
in 1940 decided that violent resistance was a necessity, a decision
which required them also to disobey the official Danish government
which for safety's sake had ordered complete passivity for the
Danish population. Of different sort, but still in the nature of
personal testimony of Thoreau's relevance to contemporary circumstance, is Professor Martin Buber's short statement entitled
"Man's Duty as Man," which identifies how and where Thoreau's
work relates to principles central in Professor Buber's existential-
ism and the philosophy of *I and Thou*.

These essays yield a harvest of insights into modern struggles
with ancient and difficult questions. What obligations does civic
responsibility impose? Must these change under different systems
of political organization? Does responsibility differ totally under
fascism or dictatorship from what it is under constitutional or
representative government? What relation does one's civic responsibility bear to the moral imperative to resist evil? Must respect
for statute law take precedence over respect for justice or for virtue? What are the sources of moral power in human beings? Where
lie the resources for moral power in government? What provision
in the social contract can be made for right of individual conscience? How is a person of conscience to act toward a government
with which he is morally at odds or it with him? Or toward a government which presumably represents a moral tradition, but from
which it has by action and sentiment veered or broken? Under
these conditions what may be the price for passivity, or for pro-

longed indecision? What function may dissent serve? What are its proper (or improper) tactics? What means of redress against tyranny do people have? What are valid grounds for the right of revolution?

Implicitly, sometimes explicitly, these essays raise such questions. Other questions, of narrower focus, force attention too. Is Thoreau's "Civil Disobedience" a practical guide to conduct in such problems? Was it written to be? Where and how has it been so used? With what consequences, what contradictions and paradoxes? In the matter of the individual's relation to the state, what constitutes a Thoreauvian standard of integrity? Are the forms of expressing such a standard static and limited? Or protean and likely to proliferate?

In the essays we have cited—by Martin Luther King, William Stuart Nelson, Martin Buber, Willard Uphaus, T. N. W. Bush, and one by a member of the Danish underground of World War II—these are not, most of them, theoretic questions safely pertaining to distant times and places. Instead, these are practical problems bound tightly to hard decisions, concrete actions, and tangible consequences. Among the answers and attitudes presented in these selections there is much agreement, but also broad and often subtle difference. The essays reward close comparison and detailed examination. They reflect live and operative forces in today's world.

The statement, for example, from the Rev. T. N. W. Bush, in the context of specific conditions in South Africa, drives forcefully to its ultimate conviction. What are moral men to do in a crisis of national life where traditional safeguards of liberty and justice (the courts, the legislature, the police, most of the press, etc.) have become in effect agents of injustice—whether by fear, policy, or gross inertia? The unflinching, perhaps prophetic, answer (and one that Bush believes Thoreau to support) is that in such circumstance men must face the necessity of active revolt "in the spirit of Harper's Ferry."

Readers who recoil from the extremity of this answer will want to read Truman Nelson's tough-minded, brilliantly illuminating essay on Thoreau and John Brown, one of the new additions to this collection. It follows in detail the absorbing drama of Thoreau's radical resolution gradually taking shape under pressure of events. It gives us a tragic, militant Thoreau sharply different from the one so often presented us in either popular myth or much of modern scholarship. Readers will also do well to remember in this context just how revolutionary traditional American doctrine actually is (that of the Declaration of Independence, for example, or of the Bill of Rights). Or to remember the variant of revolutionary logic so righteously applied at Nuremberg by American and allied prosecutors judging minor Nazi officials for concentration camp atrocities and other war crimes after World War II: i.e., obedience to murderous and enslaving edicts of state or government—whether from fear, ignorance, or misguided patriotism no matter—renders one guilty, or guilty as an accessory, to crimes against humanity. The same principle was later applied by Israelis in the trial of the notorious Eichmann at Jerusalem. It has again been invoked, this time by the Germans themselves, as recently as August 19, 1965 when the West German War Crimes Court at Frankfurt passed sentence on former staff personnel of the concentration camp at Auschwitz.

Finally, the principle that fundamental human rights must take precedence over infamous laws or policies of national governments has become an established part of the United Nations' Universal Declaration of Human Rights. (To which, incidentally, America still does not subscribe.) Thoreau's moral imperative—that non-cooperation with evil is as much a moral obligation as cooperation with good—can be said, therefore, to bear a direct relation philosophically to the progress so far made toward developing an international protection under law for the personal liberty of citizens of all countries.

Still, if Thoreau's injunction has relevance in extreme or revolutionary situations, is it not, one must ask, inapplicable to more moderate circumstances where traditional conservators of justice and liberty are not hopelessly eroded? In that case is not the effect of civil disobedience, even non-violent, ultimately to undermine a respect for law, and for essential social relationships—instead of to conserve these, or where they are weak to improve and strengthen them? Toward a reasoned judgment on such problems this gathering provides both evidence and discussion.

The essay by William Stuart Nelson deserves careful reading from those who consider Thoreau's example to be socially irresponsible, since Professor Nelson treats in detail what many overlook; that is, the specific restraints contained in "Civil Disobedience," the means cited there for preserving a respect for order even while disobeying particular laws, and Thoreau's criteria for distinguishing genuine acts of conscience from acts of mere willfulness. On the specific question of violence, Nelson sees Thoreau's attitude as essentially ambiguous—strongly influenced on the one hand by his respect for John Brown as a man of principle acting to destroy an evil system (cf. Truman Nelson's essay "Thoreau and John Brown") but counterbalanced on the other hand by his disgust of violence as it is indulged every day in a thousand petty forms by morally obtuse Americans.

As to whether the civil disobedience of Willard Uphaus, so directly inspired by Thoreau's, has had a detrimental or salutary effect upon American institutions and attitudes, perhaps a reader may himself judge. Cognizance should be taken of the tone, point, and text of the Uphaus statement before the courts; the character of those who arose to support his cause; the nature and extent of the notice the case drew not only from distinguished jurists but also from the press and from prominent religious and social organizations throughout America. One must also ask what possible benefits unrealized might have accrued if Dr. Uphaus had acted less adamantly? If he had been slower to decision? If he had given in even once to an odious injunction? Or chosen simply to set up a committee to work for the repeal of a law he despised?

Martin Luther King, it should be noted, writes advisedly of *creative* protest. The effect in America of the disobedience for which Dr. King is so prominent a symbol, the effect, that is, of disciplined non-violent demonstrations on American institutions—i.e., new federal civil-rights legislation passed, bi-racial commissions established, a new alertness and resolve imparted throughout the whole federal establishment, a new national awareness everywhere increasing—these developments argue the importance of this use of protest for helping to mobilize our resources for more equitable law and order. Where mob violence breaks out among the afflicted, is it Thoreau's tactic and the movement for civil rights that create destructive passions? Or the ugly fact that thousands of Americans know their lives (and their children's lives) to be hopeless, and their situation hopelessly unjust? Who is to say that measures already achieved from the stimulus of disobedience are not saving the country from still bloodier disruption? Without the reality of at least this relief what encouragement for restraint is there, short of brute force? Why should a desperately situated minority (equal to all in taxation, military service, and other obligations of citizenship, but unequal in housing, health, employment, schooling, voting, dignity and opportunity) be expected to endure patiently, for the so-called peace of the society, indefinite martyrdom to an afflicting *status quo?* Is it ever really in the best interest of a state that any of its citizens so sacrifice themselves? Or ask their children, and their children's children, to do so? The more especially in a nation possessing a revolutionary tradition, unparalleled affluence, and where the majority unashamedly picture themselves guardians of liberty and the pursuit of happiness in the world's citadel of democracy?

Thoreau's relevance today is most visible in such context. In either the world of the police state which dwarfs the individual and makes a cipher of him, or in that ruled by privilege and the rough justice of majority will, Thoreau is seen to inspire attitudes and to offer general strategies by which the individual, whatever his position, may at once more fully realize his dignity and potentiality as a human being; may express his moral conviction and make its power felt, if not infallibly then often with good chance for conveying this vitality undiluted into the bloodstream of community life and its institutions.

This element in Thoreau's life and work is what made so strong a personal impression upon Professor Buber. His short statement makes an excellent cross-reference to be read along with several of the essays in this gathering (Paul Lauter's "Thoreau's Prophetic Testimony" is one of these) which provide detailed discussions of individualism, symbolic act, and the power of contagion in Thoreau. As Lauter's work relates in this sense to Professor Buber's, or Truman Nelson's to T. N. W. Bush's as already noted, so in repeated instances do the selections by literary scholars and historians in this collection reinforce or take new departure from issues raised in the shorter personal statements by men of public affairs. This pattern of overlapping and extension among essays of substantially different kind and perspective imparts liveliness as well as breadth to the subject of Thoreau's political effect. In this regard, in addition to selections already mentioned, note might be taken also of Reginald L. Cook's "Think of This, Yankees!", of Leo Stoller's "Civil Disobedience: Principle and Politics," Richard Drinnon's "Thoreau's Politics of the Upright Man," C. Roland Wagner's "Lucky Fox at Walden," Theodore Baird's "Corn Grows in the Night," and Stanley Edgar Hyman's "Henry Thoreau Once More."

In the epoch of nuclear warfare, space technology, and automation, Cook and Stoller both see only a continuing relevance for Thoreau. Against threat of the nuclear count-down he is an influence forwarning that acts of intelligence and imagination must precede acts of will; he gives a rare example of moral tenacity; he is, Cook observes, "one of those intellectual antibodies in a native liberal tradition which counterattack the viral infection of economic and social injustice." Where others in this collection have emphasized Thoreau as strategist, Leo Stoller suggests that what keeps Thoreau's words permanently alive is their Promethean quality. "As long as we can hear this voice, which is timeless, we shall be certain to discover its appropriate tactics, which are of the hour." We shall be reading "Civil Disobedience" more for its spirit, then, than for its practicalities. This may seem to polish off Thoreau the tactician a little too summarily, though the point is essential for understanding one basis for Thoreau's enduring appeal. Sensing as much, Stoller emphasizes two Thoreaus: one utopian and the other political, the former an inspiration to isolated men of principle, the latter a practical man looking for allies, for ripe opportunity, and for effective means to dramatize every possible fusion of ethical principle with enlightened self-interest. Both Thoreaus have been useful in the 1960's in the campaign against racial segregation.

*6*

Stoller predicts they may eventually prove as effective in the campaign to prevent war. Cook and Stoller thus assert Thoreau's relevance to the principal problems of the mid-century. It is interesting also to see Thoreau's applicability to causes militant and pacifistic alike. This philosophical and tactical flexibility existing in one so alien to moral relativism is extraordinary. It may yet prove vital to inspiring the kind of moral resourcefulness men need for the unprecedented social problems they now face. In any case, more Americans are finding sanction in Thoreau's "Civil Disobedience" than ever before.

Richard Drinnon's "Thoreau's Politics of the Upright Man" returns us to the vexing subject of Thoreau's defiant individualism. Is it not equivalent to anarchism? Drinnon provides a review of anarchist history to show there was not a major figure in the classical background of anarchism on whom Thoreau did not draw (Sophocles' *Antigone,* for example, was an important influence). Drinnon can also make limited comparisons between Thoreau and many figures prominent in radicalism of one kind or another from the nineteenth century to the present. (His list includes Blake, Morris, Boehme, Whitman, Gandhi, Kropotkin, Alex Comfort, Emma Goldman, Isadora Duncan, Henry Miller, Albert Camus, Nicholas Berdyaev, among others.) But "anarchism" eludes precise definition; the term means all things to all people. Thoreau's fondness for irony and paradox, moreover, provides ammunition for widely divergent interpretations of his political thought.

The essentials of Thoreau's politics will not fit under abbreviated label, as Drinnon's essay goes a long way toward proving. More useful still is Drinnon's important perception that Thoreau's devastating barbs against so many existing institutions are counterbalanced by a very strong and profound community consciousness. This paradox, best reflected in Thoreau's cryptic comment that he was "as desirous of being a good neighbor as I am of being a bad subject," has not been very well understood, and constantly confuses those who see in Thoreau only the rebel against the state. Yet the point is an essential one for understanding Thoreau's relevance to modern circumstances—where perhaps only a deepening sense of community consciousness and a more sophisticated conception of world neighborliness shall deliver us from nuclear self-extermination; and where men must still learn all the arts possible for making the institution of strong central government (inseparable from industrial organization) effectively responsive to the best in human nature. Drinnon brilliantly illuminates Thoreau's service to society —*society* as something distinct from state or civil administration merely. Drinnon knows that Thoreau's ideal of freedom and naturalness never meant some condition of preliterate bliss or blind ignorance and barbaric isolation. He quotes a memorable passage from *Walden* worth our repeating.

> It is time that villages were universities, and their elder inhabitants the fellows . . . with leisure . . . to pursue liberal studies. . . . Why should our life be in any respect provincial? . . . As the nobleman of cultivated taste surrounds himself with whatever conduces to his culture —genius—learning—wit—books—paintings—statuary— music—philosophical instruments and the like; so let the villages do. . . . To act collectively is according to the spirit of our institutions. . . . Instead of noblemen, let us have noble villages of men.

On the other hand, being genuinely civilized, it is obvious, could never mean for Thoreau being subservient to authority or overlord, or being politically tamed and predictable. It was, therefore, Drinnon believes, one of Thoreau's great achievements to have gone beyond the sterile polarities of our conventional conceptions of "civilization" and "barbarism." His writings may yet by this achievement help to explode these and other oversimple political categories which paralyze political thought and social resourcefulness.

Stanley Edgar Hyman in "Henry Thoreau Once More" brings his armed vision to our collection in a discussion of recent criticism and main currents in Thoreau scholarship. His essay evaluates the principal work of this kind, but serves also as a means by which one can measure the essays contained in this volume against the major judgments elsewhere on Thoreau both past and present. Mr. Hyman uses this opportunity as well for a second look at his own previous image of Thoreau as put forth in a landmark article for the *Atlantic Monthly* in 1946. His essential Thoreau for the mid-century, now as then, remains the skillful writer showing us revolutionary truths. He agrees with F. O. Matthiessen's observation, made in 1941, that Thoreau's vitality as a revolutionary is still unexhausted.

The hazard for any collection originating as this one did, to mark a centennial year, is that tribute may tend to be merely honorific, or at worst idolatrous. But if this book honors Thoreau it does not do so uncritically. Some of the essays as already described are personal essays limited to recording, often appreciatively, how Thoreau has affected particular persons in certain times and places; general critical evaluation is not their function. But even here readers will find that strong light is not always flattering. The essay, for example, on Thoreau's importance to particular members of the Danish underground in World War II works to double effect. The writer's admiration for Thoreau is unqualified, but unqualified too is the care he takes to give utterly honest and illuminating detail; the Thoreau whom the writer sees, therefore, is not necessarily the same that some readers will see. Numerous essays in this collection deal candidly enough with various short-comings of one kind or another in Thoreau's life and personality. The angle of vision in these views also extends from political left to political right. Truman Nelson, for example, deals critically with Thoreau's obstinate individualism and with how this substantially impaired, morally as well as politically, Thoreau's radical useful-ness. Or, one of the tests of an adequate book on Thoreau, Stanley Edgar Hyman insists, is that it allow Thoreau on occasion to have acted badly, and Mr. Hyman quickly follows with some appropriate illustrations. Carl Bode's Freudian study of Thoreau, based on Raymond Gozzi's extended work of similar kind, is anything but idolatrous in its unvarnished picture of Oedipal complexities in Thoreau's psychic life.

Louise Osgood Koopman's account here of Thoreau's unsuccess-ful proposal of marriage to her mother, Ellen Sewall of Concord, is hardly a glorification of Thoreau. Indeed this delightful essay, written when Mrs. Koopman was approaching her own centenary year, derives power from its restraint and from its evocation of humble aspects of Thoreau family existence and nineteenth-century Concord life.

But place has also been made in this volume for substantial demurrer. Theodore Baird's "Corn Grows in the Night" and C. Roland Wagner's "Lucky Fox at Walden" (another essay new for this edition) both take strenuous objection to Thoreau on several grounds, and exception inevitably to many of the judgments on Thoreau put forth in other essays of this book. Our volume in this manner provides sharp internal debate, a give and take of viewpoint which the beginning student and the veteran reader of Thoreau alike can profit from following with some closeness. Professor Baird finds Thoreau far too well regarded today, the center of a cult, darling of revolutionaries and crackpots. Mr. Wagner argues Thoreau as politically naive; Baird sees him as politically pernicious when not destructive. Both find him philo-sophically confused, and flawed by an impossible egotism. Both admire him as a literary craftsman. Mr. Wagner's treatment of Thoreau and John Brown warrants comparison with Truman Nelson's, the psychoanalytic view in his essay comparison with Carl Bode's. Professor Baird's assertion of Thoreau's egotism, the affectation of God-like prescience, and the effect of this on prose style (Thoreau becomes a pretentious, paradox-moral-making bore), should be read with cross-reference to Paul Lauter's treat-ment of the same subject, or compared with Leo Stoller's comment

on the Promethean spirit in Thoreau's writing, and Thomas P. Mc-
Donnell's poem of "Buddha ensconced in a concord sky."

As some of these topics already suggest, the thematic burden
of this collection is not exclusively political, though it may be
thought predominantly so. More strictly literary considerations
beyond those mentioned are represented in Walter Harding's essay
"Five Ways of Looking at *Walden*," in C. Roland Wagner's discussion of aesthetic unity, and the lack of it, in that book. Stanley
Edgar Hyman's review of literary criticism in the field has pre-
viously been alluded to. Theodore Baird in objecting to various
non-literary uses to which Thoreau is often put urges a purely
belletristic appreciation of Thoreau and raises serious questions
about proper and improper approaches to literary lives and docu-
ments. Paul Lauter discusses at length the relation of prose style
to content and literary convention in various of Thoreau's books.

The effort to gain for this gathering first-hand witness to
Thoreau's significance for some contemporary philosophers and
men of affairs has simultaneously led to showing on modest scale
something of Thoreau's international significance. In that respect,
too, this collection on Thoreau is different from most others. With
better luck it might have been more impressively so. This is
perhaps a good point at which to speak of omissions and short-
comings.

Some aspects of Thoreau's international influence are very well
known, of course, such as that upon Gandhi in India. But details of
his significance elsewhere are in several instances less well documented. I regret intensely our failure finally to secure essays on a
number of topics. It would be useful to know more of the facts
about Thoreau's relevance for early leaders of the British Labor
movement, for example—an influence F. O. Matthiessen claimed
to have been sizable but whose estimate so qualified an authority
on British labor as Mrs. G. D. H. Cole thinks considerably ex-
aggerated. Thoreau's importance in England for Edward Carpenter
and his circle is still a subject for research. I wish greatly
that we had been successful in having from Japan a discussion of Thoreau in the light of oriental philosophy and religion,
and of Thoreau's appeal among contemporary Japanese intellectuals—a topic of special interest considering Thoreau's own
attraction to much that was oriental. There is also the subject of
Thoreau's possible importance at various times for intellectuals and
leaders of the world Jewish community, a prospect the more
tantalizing because of what is already included here from so
prominent a Jewish figure as Martin Buber. We still know little
about attitudes past or present toward Thoreau in South America.
I regret our unsuccessful though extensive effort (just prior to the
passage in Johannesburg of savagely restrictive penalties—including

death—for publication by native writers, whether printed in South Africa or abroad) to reach Chief Albert Luthuli, winner of the Nobel Peace Prize in 1962 and one of the founders of the African National Congress, who has reportedly long been a student of Thoreau's political essays. His comment, especially against the background of his political internment, might be of unusual interest. Any of these additions to our knowledge of Thoreau's international vitality would have handsomely enriched this volume.

Like a Hamlet in our tradition, Thoreau looms formidably: a figure harkening to ghosts of conscience that attest a rottenness in our midst; a man insisting that we act to remedy what is corrupt in the state of our affairs. A man not willing to put on false face, or to put away what the majority in any generation of his countrymen incline to disparage as too morbid, or too lofty, thought. He is therefore more, not less, necessary to a nation no longer pastoral and remote but a scientific and political center in the world. A difficult, sometimes rude, determined man; not always consistent, tortured sometimes by the split between an optimistic and a pessimistic view of human nature and the world. Possessing the scholar's mind and the poet's sensibility, preferring the simpler life of contemplation and philosophy, or the more cheerful one of saunterer and Concord neighbor, but under pressure of murderous events—like the American assault on Mexico and, principally, the murderous issue of human slavery—asserting himself in the politics of his day. Not very practical or efficient politically, but nevertheless acting in such a way as to give his life in the end a vast political significance. Ambiguous in his attitude toward violence, he was essentially a peaceful man valuing his rapport with nature, hesitant to act out against others his revolutionary conviction, but on the slavery question acting finally, in his profession as a writer, with courageous and passionate resolution. If a sanguine man fundamentally, also a brooding one, for periods of time withdrawn even from his closest friends. Often seen by others as spoiled and cantankerous; ambiguous in his attitude toward women; by many measures an impossible eccentric. But it remains more important, after all, that Thoreau also measures to heroic, perhaps even tragic, scale: a man whose name endures a moral symbol, whose energies have served to re-direct the course of national endeavor, and to affect the moral quality of modern history. Our perplexities about him, and with him, reveal our most significant bewilderments.

The diversity of place and circumstance from which the gatherings in this volume come, like the variety of opinion they express, gives witness to Thoreau's power to open our imagination, and to reinvigorate our sense of choice. The controversy he ignites is necessary to the economy of the self; it is not a controversy manufactured for the literary and scholarly marketplace; it is urgently internal as well as widespread. In writing of Thoreau many of the contributors to these pages confront, inevitably, their own account of "Where I Lived and What I Lived For." The reader, too, like the writer, is forced to ask: What is my life and its true necessaries? What dreams have I, and by what are they frustrated? From what sources must we, can we, derive our moral sanctions? We may, therefore, see in these pages a vital tradition working to renew, to transmit itself in present time and circumstance. "Be it life or death we crave only reality," Thoreau wrote. From this gathering we learn anew that "no method nor discipline can supersede the necessity of being forever on the alert. What is a course of history, or philosophy, or poetry, no matter how well selected, or the best society, or the most admirable routine of life, compared with the discipline of looking always at what is to be seen? Will you be a reader, a student merely, or a seer? Read your fate, see what is before you, and walk on into futurity."

# A LEGACY OF CREATIVE PROTEST

THE REV. MARTIN LUTHER KING, JR.

*During my early college days I read Thoreau's
essay on civil disobedience for the first time.
Fascinated by the idea of refusing to cooperate
with an evil system, I was so deeply moved that
I re-read the work several times. I became convinced then that non-cooperation with evil is as
much a moral obligation as is cooperation with
good. No other person has been more eloquent
and passionate in getting this idea across than
Henry David Thoreau. As a result of his writings and personal witness we are the heirs of a
legacy of creative protest. It goes without saying
that the teachings of Thoreau are alive today, indeed, they are more alive today than ever before.
Whether expressed in a sit-in at lunch counters,
a freedom ride into Mississippi, a peaceful protest in Albany, Georgia, a bus boycott in Montgomery, Alabama, it is an outgrowth of Thoreau's insistence that evil must be resisted and
no moral man can patiently adjust to injustice.*

# THOREAU AND AMERICAN
# NON-VIOLENT RESISTANCE

## WILLIAM STUART NELSON

IT IS YET TO DAWN FULLY upon the participants in sit-ins, free-dom rides and other recent forms of non-violent resistance in the United States how deeply indebted they are to Henry David Thor-eau. Thoreau's name is mentioned upon occasion. Martin Luther King recalls that early in the 1955 bus boycott of Montgomery, Alabama, he reflected on Thoreau's essay on "Civil Disobedience" and was convinced that in Montgomery he and his followers were simply making clear, in the spirit of Thoreau, that they could no longer co-operate with an evil system.

Participants in this non-violent movement acknowledge a pro-found indebtedness to Mohandas K. Gandhi. Those who have not read the following words of Gandhi would profit in so doing:

> Why, of course, I read Thoreau. I read *Walden* first in Johannesburg in South Africa in 1906 and his ideas in-fluenced me greatly. I adopted some of them and recom-mended the study of Thoreau to all my friends who were helping me in the cause of Indian independence. Why, I actually took the name of my movement from Thoreau's essay, "On the duty of Civil Disobedience," written about eighty years ago. Until I read that essay I never found a suitable English translation for my Indian word, *Satya-graha*. You remember that Thoreau invented and prac-tised the idea of civil disobedience in Concord, Massa-chusetts, by refusing to pay his poll tax as a protest against the United States government. He went to jail too. There is no doubt that Thoreau's ideas greatly in-fluenced my movement in India.*

The right to disobey government has been defended in litera-ture and in practice for thousands of years, but Americans engaged in or confronted by a civil resistance movement must above all understand Thoreau. He conceded that government is a present necessity but held that governments by their very nature are prone to err. The best of them are supported by majorities, indicating a victory of numbers and not necessarily of justice. Law makers, as Thoreau observed, too frequently serve the state with their heads and often unintentionally serve the devil. What place, we

---

* Quoted by George Hendrick, "Influence of Thoreau and Emerson on Gandhi's Satyagraha," *Gandhi Marg.*, III (July, 1959), 166.

may then inquire, is left in such a government for conscience? If it is desirable to develop a respect for law, it is essential to cultivate a respect for conscience.

A genuine non-violent movement, therefore, includes the assertion of the right of conscience in the presence of the rule of law. It is an appeal beyond government to the character of those whom the government purports to represent.

Such an appeal, if it is responsible, has its laws. Civil resistance is not necessarily invoked against every law which is regarded as bad. It is obvious that a man cannot give himself to the eradication of every wrong however great. He can, of course, dissassociate himself from it. Against what wrong of government, then, should he oppose his conscience? In "Civil Disobedience" Thoreau has a formula: "If the injustice is part of the necessary friction of the machine of government, let it go, let it go: perchance it will wear smooth—certainly the machine will wear out . . . but if it is of such a nature that it requires you to be an agent of injustice to another, then, I say, break the law. Let your life be a counter friction—friction to stop the machine. What I have to do is to see, at any rate, that I do not lend myself to the wrong which I condemn."

Civil disobedience requires also on the part of the resister the willing subjection to the penalty exacted by the law. As Thoreau states, "Under a government which imprisons any unjustly the true place for a just man is also in prison." If the place of the fugitive slave in Massachusetts is in prison, then the only place for her free and just citizens is also in the prisons. This is in token of respect for law as law. Moreover, it gives maximum force to protest, for as Thoreau points out a just minority is irresistible when it acts with its whole weight. The state will not place or keep all just men in prison. Rather than this, it will abandon its evil practice.

The discussion of the civil disobedience aspect of non-violence and non-violent resistance is of greatest importance, but it would be extremely shortsighted and superficial to conclude that the meaning of non-violence is exhausted merely by such a discussion. It is likewise unfortunate to separate Thoreau's doctrine of civil disobedience from other profound manifestations of his spirit. To persist in so doing is to miss the total message which he so forcefully epitomizes. It is only in the grasping of this total message that Negroes might possibly guarantee the fulfillment of Gandhi's fateful prophecy, namely, that it might be through them that the unadulterated message of non-violence would be made available to the world.

The roots of Thoreau's concept of civil resistance were deep. As a Transcendentalist he had turned away from economic royal-

July & August 1840.

Spes sibi quisque. Virgil.

The brave man is the elder son of creation, who steps bravantly into his inheritance, while the coward, who is the younger, waits patiently till he decease.

He is that ninth champion against Thebes, whom, when the proud devices of the rest have been recorded, the poet describes as "bearing a full-orbed shield of solid brass,"

"But there was no device upon its circle,
For not to seem just but to be is his wish."

"Discretion is the true man's soul" saith the poet. His prudence may safely go many steps beyond the utmost confines of the fool.

There is as much music in the world as virtue — At length music will be the universal language, and men greet

Thoreau's "Lost" Journal, vol. 3. Entry for July and August 1840. *Reproduced with permission of the Trustees of The Pierpont Morgan Library.*

ism and was convinced that the purest insight commonly was not to be found in the person who accumulated property. His poverty he wore as a badge of honor and he preached eloquently against materialism, the disease of his century, reminding men that they err in laying up treasures which moths corrupt.

For him, living was the precious goal and the cost of a thing was "the amount of life it requires to be exchanged for it immediately and in the long run." Rebelling against acquisition, he was happy in the gift to him by the gods of years without an encumbrance. He was willing to live so Spartan-like as to put to flight all that was not life. He journeyed to Walden Pond not, as some may think, to flee from life but in the midst of this apparent privation to find it. One is reminded of Gandhi in our own time, who insisted that in the spirit of this self-denial he must reduce himself to zero. The Christ, the Buddha—all those who have found the secret of living in its noblest flowering—have seen the wisdom of finding the self by losing it. It cannot be expected that non-violent movements will be completely manned by such spirits as these. At the center, however, there must be those selfless, disinterested standard-bearers for whom fulness of life exists apart from material possessions.

There is a further quality without which no truly non-violent movement can be built. It is compassion—not simply sorrow for the suffering man but identification with him. This is the quality that led Gandhi to adopt his scant attire when he saw a woman in her one remaining sari, the remnant of a once adequate garment, and to declare that he would wear this minimum attire until somehow no longer would a woman of India be forced to such an embarrassing estate; or led Gandhi, when he could not abolish untouchability, to adopt an untouchable as his daughter and often to elect to live among untouchables.

Some may find it difficult to associate this quality with Thoreau. It was nonetheless present. His identification with the evil linked to the extension of slavery led him to prison; his unity in spirit with John Brown enabled Thoreau to defend him in the face of bitter hostility and threatened violence. Most men saw and judged John Brown from the outside. Thoreau knew and felt him from within. When the village postmaster was reported to have said of John Brown, "He died as the fool dieth," Thoreau said he should have been answered as follows: "He did not live as the fool liveth, and he died as he lived." Thoreau declared also: "It galls me to listen to the remarks of craven-hearted neighbors who speak disparagingly of Brown because he resorted to violence, resisted the government, threw his life away!—what way have they thrown their lives, pray?—neighbors who would praise a man for attacking singly an ordinary band of thieves or murderers. Such minds are not equal to the occasion. They preserve the so-called peace of their community by deeds of petty violence every day. ... So they defend themselves and their hen roosts, and maintain slavery." Thoreau continued: "There sits a tyrant holding fettered four millions of slaves. Here comes their heroic liberator; if he falls, will he not still live?"

Thoreau saw through the crust of John Brown's violence, a violence which Brown had learned from thousands of years of pagan and Christian history and the practice of his own time. Thoreau, penetrating that crust, identified himself with the spirit of the man which sought the overthrow of an evil system.

The lesson here is that in a movement motivated by genuine non-violence, such as inspires the current resistance to racial injustice in America, men risk their lives not for beliefs but for *passionate* beliefs, beliefs in which intellectual accord has been deepened by spiritual identification.

These two threads—civil disobedience on the one hand and, on the other, capacity for divorcement from the material along with passionate identification with suffering—remained consistently interwoven throughout the life of Henry David Thoreau in spite of the urgings by others that he order his life otherwise. To illustrate, following the night in jail Thoreau completed his journey to the shoemaker interrupted by his arrest the day before. Having retrieved his shoe, he went huckleberrying. Emerson felt impatiently that Thoreau, instead of serving as the captain of huckleberry parties, should be employing his great gifts in leadership for all America. This, of course, would have proved a large responsibility even in Thoreau's and Emerson's time. Fortunately, Thoreau was not moved from his course. He remained true to himself. In our time, his life and thought, developed between and perhaps even during his jaunts through the woods in quest of huckleberries, move with increasing power upon America. Those who today assume the difficult role of removing certain of our country's weaknesses by non-violence, including civil disobedience, will do well to ponder Thoreau both as jail-goer and the voice of protest. Thoreau should also be remembered as one who resisted the temptation to permit things to ride in the saddle of his soul and who counted his life as none too precious a gift in testimony to his compassion for justice and for those who were willing to die in its behalf.

# MAN'S DUTY AS MAN

## MARTIN BUBER

Es SIND NUN NAHEZU SECHZIG JAHRE HER, dass ich Thoreaus Traktat über den "bürgerlichen Ungehorsam" kennen lernte. Ich las ihn mit dem starken Gefühl: Das ist etwas, was mich unmittelbar angeht. Erst sehr viel später aber habe ich verstanden, woher jenes Gefühl kam. Es war das Konkrete, Persönliche, das "Jetzt und Hier" an der Schrift, was ihr mein Herz gewann. Thoreau formulierte nicht einen allgemeinen Grundsatz als solchen; er beschrieb und begründete seine Haltung in einer bestimmten historisch-biographischen Situation. Er sprach seinen Leser im Bereiche dieser ihnen gemeinsamen Situation so an, dass der Leser nicht bloss erfuhr, warum Thoreau damals so handelte, wie er handelte, sondern—wofern dieser Leser nur redlich und unbefangen war—auch, dass er selber, der Leser, gegebenenfalls eben solcherweise handeln musste, wenn es ihm ernstlich darum zu tun war, seine menschliche Existenz zu verwirklichen.

Es geht hier nicht einfach um einen der vielen Einzelfälle in dem Kampf einer machtlosen Wahrheit gegen eine wahrheitsfeindlich gewordene Macht. Es geht um die ganz konkrete Aufzeigung des Punktes, an dem je und je dieser Kampf zur Pflicht des Menschen *als Mensch* wird. Indem Thoreau von seiner geschichtlichen Situation so konkret spricht, wie er es tut, sagt er das für alle Menschengeschichte Gültige auf die richtige Weise aus.

JERUSALEM, OCTOBER 15, 1962

*It is now nearly sixty years since I first got to know Thoreau's essay "Civil Disobedience." I read it with the strong feeling that here was something that concerned me directly. Not till very much later, however, did I understand the origin of this feeling. It was the concrete, the personal element, the "here and now" of this work that won me over. Thoreau did not put forth a general proposition as such; he described and established his attitude in a specific historical-biographic situation. He addressed his reader within the very sphere of this situation common to both of them in such a way that the reader not only discovered why Thoreau acted as he did at that time but also that the reader—assuming him of course to be honest and dispassionate—would have to act in just such a way whenever the proper occasion arose, provided he was seriously engaged in fulfilling his existence as a human person.*

*The question here is not just about one of the numerous individual cases in the struggle between a truth powerless to act and a power that has become the enemy of truth. It is really a question of the absolutely concrete demonstration of the point at which this struggle at any moment becomes man's duty* as man. *By speaking as concretely as he does about his own historical situation, Thoreau expresses exactly that which is valid for all human history.*

(Translated by the author)

*19*

# THOREAU AND THE DANISH RESISTANCE

## AN ANONYMOUS MEMOIR

WHAT WAS THE SPECIAL APPEAL of Thoreau's "Civil Disobedience" for some members of the Danish resistance movement during the German occupation of Denmark in the Hitler-war? Here is my personal testimony of what Thoreau meant to me as an individual during that time.

For five years, starting in April 1940, Denmark was occupied by the Nazis, in spite of an old, often renewed non-aggression pact. The occupation, unfortunately, met without appreciable resistance. The Danish government, desiring not to make matters worse, forbade resistance, commanding submission and obedience to the huge, superior German force. It was my resentment against the mean treatment of shot-down, wounded English and Canadian airmen that first forced me into the resistance.* With my knowledge of foreign languages and as a former telegraph operator in my youth, I was at once put into a team having direct communication with London for the last three years of the war.

Thoreau's "Civil Disobedience" stood for me, and for my first leader in the resistance movement, as a shining light with which we could examine the policy of complete passivity which our government had ordered for the whole Danish population. The German Wehrmacht behaved well if not provoked, but the Gestapo was boundlessly cruel. Non-violence, as a means of resistance, was completely unfit for this scum of the worst gangsters of Germany from whom they were all recruited. I lent Thoreau's books to friends, told them about him, and our circle grew. Railroads, bridges, and factories that worked for the Germans were blown up.

Since the Hitler-war, too, "Civil Disobedience" has been of very great interest for us resistance people. We are all disgusted with the seemingly endless expedience of politics, with politicians and statesmen who never have unambiguous attitudes. Integrity makes it impossible sometimes for many of us to even vote in local and general elections.

---

* In the spring of 1942 a Canadian bomber was shot down near our little town. Only one of the crew was rescued from the burning machine; unfortunately he was taken, by well-intentioned farmers, to the nearest hospital, instead of into hiding; unfortunately, because our group could have called a doctor, arranged for care, and told the Germans that the whole crew had perished. The young, lightly-wounded gunner, who had married three weeks before, implored the surgeon to inform his wife that he lived. The Germans would have taken him away the same night, but the surgeon insisted that the Canadian was too feeble to be removed. I was sent for and went to the private sick-room with the doctor past the German soldier before

## THOREAU AND THE DANISH RESISTANCE

My teacher of English as an undergraduate had learned English from a considerable philosopher, Aage Werner, the son of a rich businessman in Copenhagen. Werner was an outstanding teacher, the first Dane who used phonographic wax cylinders carrying the voices of teachers and famous actors whom he had met in London during his student years in England. Werner's textbooks are still used. He died in 1910, only forty-two years old. He was aflame with enthusiasm for Thoreau, took pride in living as simply as possible, so that his pecuniary and physical needs were minimal. He spent his great fortune to relieve the distresses of others. He never charged for his teaching, avoided "society," but spoke readily to the common man. Like Thoreau, he lived unmarried, because, as he said, "God will not revenge himself on my children unto the third and fourth generation."

Thoreau, during the thirty-seven years I have read his books, has continually influenced very deeply my conduct of life. He has increased my natural reticence towards the man in the street, whose ravenous materialism I loathe. I like to call on the man of the sea, the sailor and the fisherman. Their occasional life-and-death struggles often show us a religious instinct and a more earnest outlook than the farmer's and the townsman's.

All detestation is despicable, but since the Hitler-war I have undergone a daily inward struggle to quell a profound spite against the nation that twice in my days has set fire to the world, and now manages with one of the hardest currencies of all, wallowing in the grossest materialism.

Though I am a bad disciple of Thoreau, rather than visit the Acropolis I would go to Walden and to his grave.

---

the door, took his wife's address and promised to let her know about his fate. He wept for joy, pressed my hands and said that his burns were now less painful. A few hours later the Germans took him to their own hospital and from there to a concentration camp in North Germany. Now he lives happily in Toronto, Canada, and we still correspond.

About later air-accidents during the war I sent messages to the proper parties, acquired lifelong friends, particularly in U.S.A. (most aircraft were American) and still receive long, tragic letters from relatives who ask for details of their loved ones who crashed. I send information with photos when possible. Since the end of the war, families have continued to visit the sites of the accidents. The Danes have placed memorial stones with the names of the dead at all such sites.

# CONSCIENCE AND DISOBEDIENCE

## WILLARD UPHAUS

THE LAWN OF MERRIMACK COUNTY JAIL in New Hampshire where I was imprisoned for a year slopes gently down to the bank of the winding Merrimack River where David Henry Thoreau once paddled. Once each week I was permitted under guard to go to a nearby building on a higher level to be treated by an osteopathic physician, and as I returned to my cellblock I surveyed, for a few moments, the beautiful landscape across the valley through which the river flowed. The sight of the river, and *Walden,* one of my valued jail possessions, made Thoreau an ever-living presence. The principles enunciated in his great essay on "Civil Disobedience" helped sustain me.

The situation in which I found myself was different from that which Thoreau faced, but the basic issues were very much alike. Would I refuse to cooperate with what I believed to be morally wrong and contrary to the historic principles on which our country was founded? Thoreau had great faith in the moral and spiritual power that one honest person can wield. In "Civil Disobedience" he declared, "I know this well, if one thousand, if one hundred, if ten honest men only—ay, if one HONEST man, in this State of Massachusetts, ceasing to hold slaves, were actually to withdraw from this co-partnership, and be locked up in the county jail therefor, it would be the abolition of slavery in America." What applied to abolition of slavery when Thoreau lived, would apply in the present when the freedoms guaranteed by the First Amendment were in peril.

Like Thoreau I found my conscience coming into conflict with state authority. In 1954, at the height of the McCarthy hysteria, the State Legislature of New Hampshire authorized an inquiry by the Attorney General for the avowed purpose of disclosing activities threatening the overthrow by force and violence of the government of the United States and the State of New Hampshire. As executive director of World Fellowship Center near Conway, I was among those summoned to the inquiry. This Center, which had been in operation since 1941, as a forum-resort, is open to people of all races, faiths, nationalities and political beliefs, and its guests come from all over the United States and other parts of the world. There, through lectures and discussions on world problems, we seek to understand one another's faiths and cultures and to strengthen one another in working for peace and brotherhood.

At private hearings with the Attorney General before the trial

I had answered all questions about myself, including my religious, pacifist and political views, but had refused on the grounds of conscience to turn over to the Attorney General the guest lists for two years. I was aware, through his own admission, that a cross-index was being compiled by the Attorneys-General of 37 states of persons suspected of having "subversive" ideas, and the likelihood was that the names of World Fellowship guests would be added to it, for harassment and inquisition. Some 600 persons were involved. They were people whom I knew to be innocent, and the Attorney General offered no evidence to the contrary.

When I refused at private sessions to submit the lists, I was brought before the Superior Court of Merrimack County on January 5, 1956 and asked again whether I would comply with the Attorney General's demand. When I said "No," I was held in contempt and ordered jailed until such time as I would "purge" myself by giving the names. It was a life sentence, in effect. I held before the Justice and the people assembled a copy of the Bill of Rights and said,

> I have grown up under that, I have for years been nurtured under that. I believe in it. I am a son of American soil and I love my country; and I love this document and I propose to uphold it with the full strength and power of my spirit and intelligence. . . . In the final analysis . . . one must make up his own mind or his own heart and conscience as to what he shall do. For a year and a half the question has been before me, and my answer must be "No, Your Honor."

I could not help but feel that the Justice, also a churchman, shared my repugnance at the thought of betraying innocent people; for he said after I had completed my statement: "In substance . . . you do not want to turn informer."

The State Supreme Court upheld the lower court by a 3 to 2 decision. Later the United States Supreme Court sustained the New Hampshire courts by a 5 to 4 ruling, with Chief Justice Warren and Justices Black, Brennan, and Douglas strongly dissenting. Finally, after three years of litigation, I was once more brought before the Superior Court and given another chance to answer the question. My conscience had not changed. The sentence was not indefinite, as before, but limited to one year. I was committed on December 14, 1959.

During the days of confinement I realized how much I had been influenced by our Judeo-Christian and American heritage. Our religious tradition has characteristically despised the informer. The people of ancient Israel had been taught that "he who puts his neighbor to public shame is considered as if he had shed blood."

Professor George Williams, Harvard's church historian, points out in a paper entitled "Reluctance To Inform" that Christians before Constantine's conversion, who were often hunted down and killed, "looked upon informing as a most hazardous and odious form of defection."

This commitment to the right of conscience appeared in the early period of our country. Benjamin Ginsberg in a splendid little book entitled "Rededication to Freedom" reviews the background of our Bill of Rights and defends the indivisibility of freedom. "The American Bill of Rights," he says, "embodies the modern concept of political liberty—the concept of liberty which centers in the freedom of the moral consciousness from control by the state.... The principle of the modern libertarian state is to be found in germ in the enunciation of the Biblical maxim, 'Render therefore unto Caesar the things which are Caesar's; and unto God the things that are God's.' " In other words, the "Judeo-Christian monotheism gave to the individual perspective a sanctuary and a loyalty which transcends the tribe and nation."

There was considerable discussion of these principles during the days of the formation of the state constitutions. Theophelus Parsons, a young lawyer who helped frame the constitution of Massachusetts said,

> We have duties, for the discharge of which we are accountable to our Creator and benefactor, which no human can cancel. What those duties are is determined by right reason, which may be, and is well called an informed conscience. What this conscience dictates as our duty, is so; and that power which assumes control over it, is an usurper; for no consent can be pleaded to justify control, as any consent in this is void.

The framers of the New Hampshire Bill of Rights actually accepted this principle when they adopted Article 4 which reads, "Among the natural rights, some are, in their very nature, unalienable, because no equivalent can be given or received for them. Of this kind are the rights of conscience." It was New Hampshire's own Daniel Webster who declared, "The contest for ages has been to rescue liberty from the grasp of executive power."

In May, 1960, Dean Erwin N. Griswold of the Harvard Law School said when speaking at the Centennial of The Law School of Northwestern University in Chicago, that "The right to be let alone is the underlying theme of the Bill of Rights. It has continued to be fertile soil for the cultivation of individual freedom."

As Americans, Thoreau and I leaned on the same tradition. "That government is best which governs not at all; and when men are prepared for it, that will be the kind of government they will have," he declared. My own conscience told me that the Attorney

General was exercising authority under the law that was leading to the destruction of our civil and religious liberties, the weakening of the Bill of Rights, and bringing harm to innocent people. The state's anti-subversive law was being used to snoop into men's thoughts and interfere with their lawful associations. The legislators who passed the law were men who, it seemed to me, were well described by Thoreau as men who do not serve their state "as men mainly, but as mechanics, with their bodies." They engage in "no free exercise whatever of the judgment or of the moral sense."

Thoreau argued that it is sometimes necessary to stand alone. He applied the principle of civil disobedience when he condemned Abolitionists for not at once withdrawing effectually their support, "both in person and property, against the government of Massachusetts." They were not to wait till "they constitute a majority of one, before they suffer the right to prevail through them." "I think," he said, "it is enough if they have God on their side, without waiting for that other one. Moreover, any man more right than his neighbor constitutes a majority of one already."

Again, "A government in which the majority rule in all cases cannot be based on justice, even as far as men can understand it. Can there not be a government in which majorities do not virtually decide right and wrong, but conscience. . . . Must the citizen even for a moment, or in the least degree resign his conscience to the legislator? Why has every man a conscience, then? I think we should be men first and subjects afterward. It is not desirable to cultivate respect for the law, as much as for the right. The only obligation which I have a right to assume is to do at any time what I think right."

There was an all-outness about Thoreau. He had contempt for the mere amelioration of wrong. For Thoreau reforms "take too much time and man's life will be gone." "Cast your whole vote, not a strip of paper merely, but your whole influence," he insisted. "Action from principle, the perception and the performance of right, changes things and relations; it is essentially revolutionary, and does not consist wholly with anything that was."

I felt, therefore, that Thoreau would have supported me in my full non-cooperation with what I believed to be bad law, even if it meant prison. This was better than to have given in just once, to have exposed innocent persons to harassment and persecution, and then to have salved my conscience by setting up a committee to work for the repeal of the law. The truth is that the image of the "frail old man," built up by the newspapers, set forces loose far beyond the expectation of the politicians who sought to humiliate me and, if necessary, put me behind bars. The Emergency Civil Liberties Committee took up the case. The newly founded Religious Freedom Committee informed the clergy of the nation on the issues. Many religious bodies passed strong resolutions. Local defense committees sprang up. Organizations like the Liberal Citizens of Massachusetts entered the fight. Letters by the hundreds were written to the papers, to the Governor of New Hampshire, the Attorney General and the judge who committed me. Many religious journals spoke out. Great American dailies like *The New York Times, The Washington Post, The St. Louis Post-Dispatch, The Christian Science Monitor,* and *The Providence Journal* editorialized. Guests flocked to World Fellowship with a new loyalty. I was able at the end of the year to emerge victorious, and able to say I had peace in my heart, first because I had stood firm, and second, because I held no hate in my heart against any human being.

The days in prison were for me, above all else, a time for reviewing a treasury of memories and associations, and of evaluating the years that had passed. I knew that conscience was not a miracle. Mine was an American conscience fed from childhood by the moral imperatives of a stern but tender upbringing, and by life on the land where I felt rapport with all living things. I saw more clearly what had been the effect, in my twenties, of teaching high school courses in English Literature when I drank deep of the American tradition embodied in the essayists and poets of early New England. The words of Ralph Waldo Emerson took root and grew in my mind: "The one thing in the world of value is the active soul,—the soul, free, sovereign, active. This every man is entitled to; this every man contains within him, although in almost all men obstructed. . . ." Studying and teaching Thoreau, I learned anew the great lesson of the Declaration of Independence that authority must be resisted if its demands violate conscience.

Later, during my four years of graduate study at Yale University Divinity School, I was physically as well as spiritually at home in the environment that had given birth to the heritage that had so taken hold of me.

Finally, at one point, I am not sure whether I understand Thoreau or enter into his experience. I believe with him, with my whole heart, in the power of the *one,* but I cannot follow, without question, his belief that "there is little virtue in the masses of men." How can I separate the *one* from the *many?* The *ones* are sometimes the projection of the unspoken hopes and consciences of the *many.* I cannot think of the *one* as a leader apart. Is he simply leading, or is he being thrust forward? I cannot speak of my own experience—the long years of legal struggle and the year of imprisonment—without becoming eloquent about the everlasting "we," knowing that any moral and political victory was won through the sacrifice and prayerful efforts of the many.

# THOREAU IN SOUTH AFRICA

## A LETTER FROM THE REV. TREVOR N. W. BUSH

To John H. Hicks:

*Your letter, addressed to me at St. Andrew's College, Minaki, Tanganyika, reached me last week. As you know, I left South Africa as a political refugee after assisting the banned African National Congress to organize demonstrations of protest against the apartheid policies of the government. After spending a short time in East Africa I proceeded to Europe during March. At present I am working in a Welsh industrial parish but I expect to take up a teaching appointment in Cardiff during September.*

*I am deeply moved by your request for a tribute to Henry David Thoreau. His influence in South Africa has been extremely important and our struggle to win rights for the oppressed non-white population of our country has been assisted profoundly by the fearless liberal teachings and example of your great philosopher and prophet. It is therefore with pride that I wish to be associated with those who pay tribute to him during this one hundredth anniversary of his death.*

*If Thoreau were alive today he would certainly join forces with those who resist racial intolerance and the evils which flow from it. He would recognize, as we do, that although "the four million slaves" have been emancipated, many more millions of dark-skinned people continue to suffer unspeakable misery and indignities at the hands of allegedly Christian and democratic white people. Like the immortal John Brown who is the subject of so much of his writing, his example would be "to face his country herself, when she was in the wrong." We must not forget the courage which enabled him to campaign actively against slavery, the Mexican War, and the dispossession and despoiling of Indians. How much more would he direct his anger against the new and more diabolically subtle forms of slavery of the twentieth century, whether they take the guise of apartheid, Southern segregation, or the exploitation of people through neo-colonialism!*

*It is also opportune that we should remember Thoreau's attacks upon national leaders, pressmen and church dignitaries who failed to give a lead in the struggle for justice: "Those who, while they disapprove of the character and measures of a government, yield to it their allegiance and support, and are thus undoubtedly its most conscientious supporters, and so frequently the most serious obstacles to reform." Talking and writing about abuses is not enough, he said, and there are times when it is patriotic to rise up in active revolt against a system which permits and encourages injustice by inertia and inaction. "The spirit of Harper's Ferry" must never be forgotten by those who are called to be reformers of the national life.*

*Recent history and the present time have produced campaigners for justice of Thoreau's calibre. Many have been profoundly influenced by his writings and can attribute their success in part to his compelling and inspiring lead. Gandhi, Martin Luther King, Albert Luthuli belong to this company, men who have sacrificed comfort and material advancement to win recognition for the rights of their fellow-human beings. Like Thoreau they are fearless of the unpleasant labels their enemies have attempted to attach to them, and of the venomous retaliations of those whose selfish interests their activities have threatened.*

*I congratulate you on your plans to draw renewed attention to this outstanding American. Please accept my sincere good wishes and my earnest hope that you will succeed in persuading people in countries all over the world to take courage and inspiration from the message and work of your great fellow-citizen.*

T. N. W. Bush
*June 13, 1962*

# THINK OF THIS, YANKEES!

## REGINALD L. COOK

THOREAU IS AN ORIGINAL SHOT still heard echoing around the world. Wherever Jefferson's inalienable rights are in doubt, Thoreau confirms these rights. If the Ironist, Circumstance, makes a fool of our best purposes and life runs to things, he is there to reprove us with a principle and a method by which human values can be realized. If the right of human liberty is withheld, his courageous conviction exposes the denial as a last refinement of human injustice, whether in American courtrooms, in a rural commune system, or in foreign concentration camps. He would have changed the indicative to the conditional mode in President Kennedy's statement: "The one great irreversible trend in world history is [should be] on the side of liberty—and so, for all time to come are we." If, in our pursuit of happiness, the moment of the countdown in nuclear warfare haunts us, he has forewarned us that acts of intelligence and acts of imagination must precede acts of will. Time runs out; there is no thirteen o'clock. But this is not to say the muzzle velocity of his shot would be any less diminished as it hits the status-seekers, the organization men, and the arrogant suspicions of the illiberal John Birch Society.

In this epoch of nuclear energy, missile propulsion, space-and-under-sea technology, electronics and automation, I see only a continuing relevance in Thoreau. But does this relevance elevate the symbolic Thoreau or the masterly prose writer? A spiny Yankee no less than tangy prose are at the root of my devotion. One of the most important personal facts in my life is Henry Thoreau. I am not at all sure I know him, and I haven't the slightest desire to pluck the heart of his mystery, if it were possible. If only I can see a little more clearly the significance of what he stands for each time I read him, this would constitute my desideratum. We grow into the classics; they are not to be taken by assault. And *Walden* is one of the classics in which an act of life is translated into an act of imagination.

Born about thirty miles south of Concord, I first read *Walden* as a college sophomore, and I have never relinquished a passionate interest in both the man and the book, varying in intensity and emphasis with the occasion. Periods of substantial demurrer followed periods of uncritical agreement. Melville did not want to oscillate in Emerson's rainbow, and Emerson himself has warned us about being warped clear out of our orbit by another man's thought. Neither have I wanted to be less than my own man in my own time. After a foreign sojourn I returned to teach in Middlebury College, my alma mater, and Thoreau was one of the classic American writers I was under compulsion to teach and interpret to the students in the twentieth century. This is a greater challenge than might appear. A Coleridgean "film of familiarity" can preclude not only accurate insight but genuine feeling about the books we teach. Our danger is superficiality, not insincerity. How, then, do I take him? First, as a man of his own time—a transcendental idealist.

"The best of the Americans are mystics by instinct," said D. H. Lawrence. A transcendental "Walker, Errant," Thoreau differs from Emerson's hearthstone mysticism less in high-minded austerity than in *practical* idealism. He was more firmly rooted in American earth. Only his sensibility was swept by the transcendental tune of the times. His cleaving intellect both naturalized and domesticated him. "Of thee, O earth, are my bones and sinews made. . . . Here have I my habitat. I am of thee." Which points up his exception to the Laurentian contention that Americans "have never loved the soil of America as Europeans have loved the soil of Europe."

The dominant image in Thoreau's life is the journey. His *Journal,* a record of an interior life, is a pilgrim's progress. As a hunter of the beautiful his quarry was a transient thought, vision or dream. Indeed his inveterate journeying seems far more allegorical than actual. Although the object of the search might be the beautiful purple azalea, the search itself was like a passage in a myth. Consequently, the quotient is the extraction of the mythologic from such natural phenomena as the emperor moth's cocoon on the scrub apple tree, or the sight of the sucker floating on the meadow stream, or the lesser redpolls seen in a winter landscape. He felt serene and satisfied when the events of the day had "a mythological character, and the most trivial is symbolical." For example, when he returned from a walk on January 1, 1854, he recorded in the *Journal* with transcendental exultation: "Did this great snow come to reveal the track of some timorous hare, or of the Great Hare, whose track no hunter has seen?"

The trait which defines the special Thoreauvian quality is the relentless exercise of moral will in pursuit of a goal. Imagine what an act of will it takes to tramp "eight or ten miles through the deepest snow to keep an appointment with a beech-tree, or a yellow birch, or an old acquaintance among the pines . . . wading to the tops of the highest hills when the snow was nearly two feet deep on a level. . . ." The Puritan strain of moral zeal identifiable with the early Christian soldiers survives in the romantic temperament of this Yankee. Thoreau's method is a naturalist's, but his effects are those of a transcendental poet. In an age of romantic symbolism, when every thicket might be a burning bush, he only sojourned in civilization. There is, in consequence, much of the mythologic in his heuristic absorption with the redpolls, the emperor moth cocoons, the ring of "white and slumbering" phosphorescent light in a piece of rotten moose-wood, the purple azalea, the Norway cinquefoil, or the floating sucker. Every incident was a parable of the Great Teacher. Isn't this partly what his sister meant when she referred to the impression her brother's life made upon her as "a grand miracle"? Did he not dream recurrently of climbing a mountain, passing through the dark woods, going clear to the top? Did he not climb Wachusett, Katahdin and Monadnock? Was he not at times elevated on Pisgah? Did he not sometimes see transcendentally?

Thoreau as a transcendental idealist is, then, the first of three ways in which I take him. But in arraigning the tyrannies of the state and indicting a technological civilization, I also see him as an embattled Concorder enlisted in Emerson's "soldiery of dissent." A man of conscience, his boiling point was subversion of independence. So he struck out at economic and social conformity in *Walden,* at the tyranny of the state in "Civil Disobedience," at human servitude in "Slavery in Massachusetts", at acquisitive materialism in "Life Without Principle." Today he would be concerned with the evidences of injustice and moral failure in price-fixing by large corporations, in the segregation issue and juvenile delinquency, in municipal and sports corruption, in the suppression of civil liberties and intimidation by violence. He would expect as little from the reforms which come from underlings as of the reform of the Overlords. Effective reform like Thoreau's is inward, is self-reformation. It is a disturbing truth that the Red Dwarf who unhorses us at the tourney and for whom we search everywhere is to be found only within ourselves. Nor is the road to Damascus everyman's highway.

Thoreau's radicalism is moral and ideal. His theory rests on the assumption man is a moral animal, who operates by a moral principle established on divine sanctions. His romantic imagination conceived an ideal world. Man as a free agent repudiates expediency in facilitating advantageous ends at the expense of the welfare of others. Our sober judgment tells us this is the way it ought to be, but unfortunately this is not the way it is in our kind of world. Notional and perverse, or prickly and acerbic as Thoreau is, he is also a man of great courage and conviction. Did he not ring the Concord court bell in 1844 on the occasion of Emerson's speech on emancipation in the West Indies? Did he not go to jail in 1846 for refusing to pay a tax which would support slavery? Did he not defy the Fugitive Slave Act of 1851 by aiding Negroes to escape to Canada? Did he not stand up for John Brown at a most unpopular time while the latter was still in jail? And did he not on October 30, 1859 ignore the Abolitionists who thought "it was premature and not advisable," by summoning his fellow citizens to hear his address on Captain Brown?

This side of Thoreau affects me strongly. He is one of those intellectual antibodies in a native liberal tradition which counterattack the viral infection of economic and social injustice, and which take a formidable stand in opposition to inertial conformity. It would be inexact, however, to call him a depreciator of material progress. He warned against an improved means to an unimproved end. Yet he did not fail to see the real point at issue. True enough, our washers, dryers, freezers, electrical can-openers, and garbage disposal units are improved means. Meanwhile our moral resources become blunted by our "pretty toys." The way out of this dilemma is to master the mechanical servants and make them serve strictly human ends. "If we are to live in the [twentieth] century, why should we not enjoy the advantages which the [twentieth] century offers?"

A third way I take Thoreau is by studying out the stubborn conflict between the passion of the poet for an intimate rapport with nature and the response of a conscientious man to the exacting discipline of the systematic naturalist. As early as 1851, when he was thirty-four, it distressed him to think he was becoming more scientific and narrowed down to the field of the microscope. "I see details, not wholes nor the shadow of the whole. I count some parts, and say, 'I know.'" Eight years later he wrote: "If you would make acquaintance with the ferns you must forget your botany." His fear was justified. Year by year the *Journal* tallies more natural facts and less reflective comment. He was never to forget his botany, measuring-tape, and vasculum. A sometime herbalist, entomologist, meteorologist, climatologist, agrologist, and, in the study of Walden Pond, one of our first limnologists, the fact is he was neither a well-trained nor a wholly effective systematic naturalist. When, in 1857, he deprecated the scientist's mistake in failing to relate to himself the phenomenon which excited him, he underscored his own shortcoming as a scientist and the felicity of his poetic sensibility.

The contrary pulls between the poet and the naturalist were never satisfactorily resolved any more than the beauty and romance of the river and the exact science of steamboating were in Mark Twain. A plaintive note similar to Thoreau's is heard in *Life on the Mississippi* when Mark Twain tells us how "all the grace, the beauty, the poetry, had gone out of the majestic river" as he learned to master the exact science of piloting a steamboat. "No, the romance and beauty were gone from the river. All the value any feature of it had for me now was the amount of usefulness it could furnish toward compassing the safe piloting of a steamboat." In spite of the important study of the succession of forest trees or his "lake country" limnology, the more important aspect of reality to Thoreau was subjective. Nothing is more informative in this respect than his reaction to a winter sunset. "I witness a beauty in the form or coloring of the clouds which addresses itself to my imagination, but do not so account to my imagination," he explains. "It is what it suggests and is the symbol of that I care for, and if, by any trick of science, you rob it of its symbolicalness, you do me no service and explain nothing." Standing twenty miles away, he had seen a crimson cloud on the horizon. To the scientist it would represent a mass of vapor absorbing all other rays and reflecting redness, but to an ardent romantic sensibilitist the red vision excited and stirred the blood and made his thoughts flow. The *Journal* is filled with similar responses which run the gamut of the senses. Whether it is the sight of the great fringed orchid or Indian grass, the smell of spicy-scented ants or pennyroyal, the sound of woodthrush or bittern, the taste of birch sap or wild apples, the touch of mullein leaves or goldenrod, he rejoices. Nothing natural is alien to him.

Thoreau's reputation rests on one book, and Robert Frost reminds us that some part of nearly all Thoreau had to say is in *Walden.* So it is. Here is the transcendental exponent of high thinking and plain living. "Not till we are lost, in other words not till we have lost the world, do we begin to find ourselves, and realize where we are and the infinite extent of our relations." In my early reading Walden was a place-name and an act. Later, it became a symbolic Thoreauvian state of mind in which I found an answer to Ellery Channing's disquieting perplexity about never being able to understand what Thoreau meant by his life. The question *Walden* asks is simply: how much so-called civilization is really necessary? Simplify, it says, and keep your accounts on your thumb nail. Don't be possessed by your possessions. Save on the lower levels so you can spend on the higher. Cultivate the simple but regenerating virtues of sincerity, faith, and innocence.

Here is also the social and economic critic. "While civilization has been improving our houses, it has not equally improved the men who inhabit them." Thoreau extricated himself from a social and economic predicament by temporary sequestration. The account is of a retreat and sojourn which has nothing to do with alleged escapism. In his "life in the woods" he was not following the line of least resistance but, like the bream in the Musketaquid, he was making his way upstream toward the source by *resisting* the current. The current had set toward gregariousness in urban developments, toward commerce in the extension of the factory system, and toward acquisitiveness in the Westward Movement. In his conspicuous frugality he represents a standing reproach to

America's lost innocence. In his correspondence with nature he was a ready witness. He had been there many times.

Here is also the poetic naturalist, who, standing on the pond, cuts his way through a foot of snow, another foot of ice, and opens a window under his feet "into the quiet parlor of the fishes" where "a perennial waveless serenity reigns as in the amber twilight sky, corresponding to the cool and even temperament of the inhabitants. Heaven is under our feet as well as over our heads." Were it not for the writing it is unlikely I would read *Walden* at least once a year in a kind of ritual ceremony. I read it for the same reason Marcel Proust from his cork-lined room in the Faubourg St. Germain urged the Comtesse de Noailles to read it. "Read the admirable pages of *Walden*," he wrote. "It seems to me that one reads them in oneself because they come from the depths of our intimate experience." Thoreau resembles one of Schiller's poets who "are Nature," not one of those who merely "seek her." *Walden* confirms the consonance between a man and his natural world. It is not hauteur but the confidence of rapport which prompts Thoreau to assert, "I go and come in Nature with a strange liberty, a part of herself." In his cosmic provincialism what triumphal entrances he made into Becky Stow's swamp and what grand tours of the Easterbrook country. His writings are the classic account; classic, in William Carlos Williams' terms, of "the local, fully realized, words marked by a place." This defines the special quality of *Walden*, his masterbook, where man meets nature on the level of greatest credit to each and, by memorably expressing this relationship, Thoreau is the most effective nature writer we have yet produced.

"Great writing," says Ezra Pound, "is simply language charged with meaning to the utmost degree." In *Walden* the language carries the charge. In its variety alone it is notable. It has paradoxes and metaphors, epigrams and analogies, allusions and lyrical apostrophes. The impression it makes upon me is of a writer at the top of his form with his faculties in full play. "The Fiend is party to every work of art," says Blake. Thoreau's fiend is here a sly and taunting humor. "I believe that men are generally still a little afraid of the dark, though the witches are all hung, and Christianity and candles have been introduced." "I have never yet met a man who was quite awake. How could I have looked him in the face?" Thoreau was, like Emerson, a master of the perky, straight-backed, quotable sentence. "Old deeds for old people, and new deeds for new." "From the hearth the field is a great distance." "We know but few men, a great many coats and breeches." "The civilized man is a more experienced and wise savage." They pop all over the page like corn in a popper.

Eloquence is the enforcement of a truth, a belief or an opinion, by language. Thoreau has this kind of eloquence, when, in "Spring," he describes the flight of " a very slight and graceful hawk," in a perfectly admirable passage, with the proper pitch and resonance, slowly modulated and full of lyric energy. The hawk is seen and realized in itself, related only to the sky (height), air (in suspension), and light (of day), and with no hint of man's moral superiority to it, or of its moral superiority to man. "Sporting with proud reliance in the fields of air," this hawk—Merlin, he calls it—"was not lonely, but made all the earth lonely beneath it." This is the aesthetic pleasure which *Walden* generates.

Equally impressive is the intellectual. I am impressed by the way Thoreau takes his fate and loves it—*amor fati*. He admitted, "I love *my* fate to the core and rind, and could swallow it without paring, I think." A deservedly much-quoted passage from the second chapter of *Walden* states his purpose, to front only the essential facts of life and if they turn out to be mean *or* sublime, then publish a true account, which is precisely what he did. Sophia tells of a consoling friend visiting her brother's death-bed and saying: "Well, Mr. Thoreau, we must all go." To which Thoreau replied: "When I was a very little boy I learned that I must die, and I set that down, so of course I am not disappointed now. Death is as near to you as it is to me." This death-bed rejoinder makes the eloquence of *Walden* valid. Thoreau had not only a stoical sense of human limits but a sense of possibility within limits. He could see a wider world than Concord no matter how great his attachment to the latter. Just as he was able to see "an animal health and vigor distinct from the spiritual." One day he picked up the lower jaw of a hog and noticed the whiteness of the teeth and the soundness of the tusk. "This creature succeeded by other means than temperance and purity," he thought. When the tadpoles were gobbled up by the herons, he was assured, just as Whitman had been in "This Compost," of "the strong appetite and inviolable health of Nature." Thoreau reflected, "The impression made on a wise man is that of universal innocence."

Finally, there is the psychological interest which Thoreau generates in *Walden*. The most quietly moving passages are unselfconscious transparencies; for instance, the morning of contemplation, spent sitting in the sunshine on his doorstoop, absorbed in a reverie. Even as he describes it he seems not to be addressing his reader directly but simply communing. How intensely social are those who communicate in silence! Dostoevsky's Kirillov tells Stavrogin in *The Possessed:* "There are moments, you reach moments, and time suddenly stands still and it will become eternal." These "still moments" far from indicating a lethargy of human will suggest the eternal order of time in which Thoreau fished for realities. It is not quite Eliot's still point in a turning world but a burning point in a still world. Ernest Hemingway's "reality" has a sensuous quality—what tastes or looks or feels good. Thoreau's "reality" has a moral quality—the quality of *being*. So with confidence he says, "I realized what the Orientals mean by contemplation and the forsaking of works."

Thoreau knew it appeared trivial to some of his neighbors, as it did to him (transiently), to pursue a non-conformistic trial by existence. He knew too the stick we are beaten with is economic necessity, but he also knew the stick we beat ourselves with is self-doubt. He knew fate is no respecter of our condition, human or inhuman, and that the heaven of orthodoxy is haunted by consolatory Christian memories and hell by the fatalism of the despondent. Americans are notably self-improvers, and this ingenious Yankee found that by living a life of "voluntary poverty," it is possible to practise spiritual prudence. Realizing this he became self-emancipated, even from the inexorable daily round of self where our introspection is the feet we walk on. "As I was leaving the Irishman's roof after the rain, bending my steps again to the pond, my haste to catch pickerel, wading in retired meadows, in sloughs and bog-holes, in forlorn and savage places, appeared for an instant trivial to me who had been sent to school and college," he confessed in "Baker Farm," "but as I ran down the hill toward the reddening West, with the rainbow over my shoulder, and some faint tinkling sounds borne to my ear through the cleansed air, from I know not what quarter, my Good Genius seemed to say,— Go fish and hunt far and wide day by day,—farther and wider,— and rest thee by many brooks and hearth-sides without misgiving." The truth of the matter is—or the twentieth century is dead wrong —Thoreau's apparent trivialism endured to wisdom.

*Walden's* appeal can be summed up in one word: simplicity. There is little in it a big advertising agency with well-trained publicists could advantageously spend its promotional enterprise on; nothing big and resplendent, only a hut in the woods and a man with ideas. Contrasting sharply with "the billion-dollar speed-up," as Dos Passos characterizes contemporary history, there is such quietness a contemplative man could *hear* the sumac in its urgent growth and the sound of church bells from surrounding towns, which acquire a vibratory hum "as if the pine needles in the horizon were the strings of a harp which it swept." Here there is little of excitation which the lens of a TV camera might focus on, except the embattled ants when overseen in their fierce factional warfare, or the antic loon playing a whimsical game of checkers with a man in a boat on the surface of a pond on a late fall day.

*Walden* has been misinterpreted as a popular American do-it-yourself fable. Just as the large oratorical flourish of Whitman in *Leaves of Grass* has degenerated into the unaccomplished sound effects of the San Francisco "Beats," similarly Thoreau's effective parleying of a small gesture at Walden Pond into a universally recognized act degenerates into al fresco supper parties of the cook-out crowd. In view of the original experiment all imitation smacks of amateurism. How many ersatz Waldens there have been! The misinterpreted letter was substituted for the austerity of the spirit. The true *Walden* is best defined in a French physiologist's contention. "The stability of the interior environment is the condition of free life," says Claude Bernard. This inner stability is what Melville meant in *Moby Dick* by "one insular Tahiti, full of peace and joy," Hemingway by Nick Adams' fishing-camp on "the big two-hearted river," and Robert Frost in his retiring place in "Directive" where you drink at the brook, to be made "whole again beyond confusion." *Walden* is a symbolic point of vantage from which the stability of an interior environment is realized. In our time, as Mark Schorer has said, "the rebel, for so many generations the hero, disappears with his role; what we have instead is 'the stranger,' the outsider, the alienated and disaffected wanderer, the human being who declines to participate in the human enterprise." Thoreau represents neither the alienated man nor the disaffected wanderer but the "perspectival" (Nietzsche's word) self-determinationist. As an activist, he invokes an affirmative image. "We should," he said, "impart our courage and not our despair, our health and ease, and not our disease." So he does; he is eupeptic.

A tough but lucky individualist, he escaped by his wits from being ground "at the mills of the philistines." He was lucky in enjoying a sympathetic family solidarity, in revelling in an attachment to a congenial if tame natural environment, lucky in having acquired an intellectual discipline in reading and writing at Harvard, lucky in Emerson's stimulation but luckiest of all in possessing a lively sensibility which responded with hair-trigger intensity to the world ideas of his time. But he was more than lucky. He was a determined man, victimized neither by necessity, nor by personal indulgence. He worked hard to keep his broad margin. He stayed loose, as they say. And he wore his liberty cap with a difference; so different, in fact, he has encouraged many, time out of mind, to be large owners if not in the Merrimack, at least in their own, intervales, and to spend, say, twelve hours of genial converse, if not with the leopard frog, perhaps with an equally interesting subject. If Thoreau were part of the contemporary scene he would be standing up in meeting to be counted, to tell us how we might find effective self-reformation "by truly Indian, botanic, magnetic, or natural means." He would be saying it so you could hear him, just as he did in *A Week:* "Think of this, Yankees!"

# HOW IT, SO HELP ME, WAS

*JOSEPH LANGLAND*


When I first went to Walden Pond
Alone in the afternoon of the last day of summer
In the centennial of his death
The woods rang with sparrows, squirrels and crows.
Turning around the rockpile of Thoreau's hut
I discovered, also, that I had been born
In the centennial of his birth.
There in the lifted day, Icarian bird,
I circled the dark edge of an ancient dream
And started down to the water.

And the very first person I met upon my path
Was a tall young Negro.
He stood easily by the woodsy pond
With his white girl friend,
Casually linking their hands by a leaning birch.
Its leaves quivered in a light breeze
Wakening over the dark waters,
And under the random clouds in the deep sky
We smiled, and I went on.

And the very next person I met upon that path
Was a brown man from India
Lounging in mottled pebbles and blond sand
With a college sweatshirt hung on his shoulders.
Into the lake he dipped his golden hands;
He turned his palms in the common water
And lifted them, all spangled.
In the mystical geometry of light
Drops fell in a chain
And linked their circular furrows on the pond.
A frog plunked from the bank;
An autumn leaf swung down.
A bluejay screamed;
We smiled, and I went on.

And further along the brightly shadowed woods
The very next person I met upon that path
Was a wild white man
Running and leaping through the brush,
Mumbling some half-hummed song as he ran.
His jacket was flung open;
His face shone with light;
And a rumpled paisley muffler of rainbowing colors
Trailed from his torn pocket
And waved
In floating arcs among the aisles of trees,
Frightening the song sparrows into sudden answers
As he fled on.

And then, at a further turn, I met myself.
I smiled and stepped to the tall and weedy shades
At the small bay on the western edge,
Stripped to my native self
On brackish ground and shining sand
And, walking into the sun from tufted sedge
Past polliwogs and mudflats and water-spiders,
I strode those slippery shoals to the clear blue
And dove in calm delight
To thrash my limbs and throw my pale white arms
Around those springing waters.

Seeing the afternoon break from the woods
I heard the long dark tale of history flashing down
And rose in a clear dream.
Simply jeweled with all that pond
I put my homely raiment on
And rode the luminous hum of blue-grey twilight home.

# CIVIL DISOBEDIENCE:
## PRINCIPLE AND POLITICS

### LEO STOLLER

How DOES IT HAPPEN that more Americans are finding sanction in Thoreau's "Civil Disobedience" today than ever before? Let me say immediately that the answer applicable to the Negro freedom movement will not work for the peace demonstrations. The two great moral issues of our day have not yet fused. Stand at one focus and the American ellipse looks one way. Stand at the other and it looks very different. The fight to end segregation sees conditions that dictate non-violent resistance and discovers support that can make this strategy large-scale and successful. The fight to prevent war sees itself isolated from all social power and falls back on scattered individuals willing to stand witness for peace. Henry Thoreau's essay has support and lessons for both.

When Thoreau was a young man—he turned twenty-nine the year he spent that night in jail—the nation was also faced with two moral issues. In the South, white planters had for a long time been owning black laborers and using them like draught animals. In the North, factory owners were beginning to hire large numbers of wage-workers and treat them only a little better. The eighteen-fifties would separate these two issues and show that the older one would have to be resolved first and the newer wait out its maturity. Wendell Phillips gave thirty years to abolition and then turned to the eight-hour day. But in 1846 the priorities were still unclear. One aspect of Thoreau's civil disobedience that year was an effort to meet both issues through a single action.

Thoreau was at Walden Pond in the one-room house he had built with his own hands. He had moved in on the Fourth of July, declaring his independence of a culture that gave itself to owning people and things rather than to cultivating its mind and spirit. His strategy was what some have since called the one-man revolution. To change the world about him he changed himself, hoping that others would follow suit.

There were two premises behind his action. The first was that his own imagination could map out an ideal humanity. He was not the only one, of course, to work from this axiom. Some of his contemporaries discovered that a good man must never use violence or must never handle money or must never eat meat. Thoreau was not a non-resistant or a no-money man, and he wavered on vegetarianism. His good man did this: he refused to own slaves or be a slave, he refused to hire labor or hire out for labor, he stayed out of organizations, he worked the soil with his own hands, he minimized his need for food, clothing and shelter, he gave as much time as possible to his special creative impulse, and he disowned the state that administered slavery and hire and acquisitiveness.

The second premise was that American society as it stood in the mid-forties gave no hint of ever becoming better. It might help show you what your ideal humanity would not be like. But there was no path toward that ideal within it. The only way to begin changing society was to come out of it and revolutionize yourself.

But the nation did grow better. In the end the North did force the Southern whites to give up slavery. We see this easily now after the fact. Something in Thoreau had already responded to it when the fact was still gestating. If one aspect of his civil disobedience was come-outer and perfectionist, there was a second aspect that was quite different. It was not utopian but political. It stayed inside the social order, separating the ripe issue from the unripe, looking about for allies who would help change what could then be changed. It formulated no ideal personality but waited for the time to precipitate its own representative man. The contrast between the two aspects is best seen at their limits. Thoreau at twenty-nine refused to pay his tax, Thoreau at forty-four supported the government and armies of Lincoln. The younger man's hero was himself or perhaps that other refuser, Bronson Alcott. The older man's hero was Captain John Brown.

Underpinning both aspects, making them one structure, was Thoreau's bedrock radicalism. It was this that gave his essay on "Civil Disobedience" its spirit. It is not strategies, after all, that keep his words alive, it is the Prometheus in them, Shelley's Prometheus, who will never make peace with an overlord. As long as we can hear this voice, which is timeless, we shall be certain to discover its appropriate tactics, which are of the hour.

In 1846 and 1847 it looked as if a single tactic could satisfy both the utopian and the political in Henry Thoreau. Denying Massachusetts its tax and taking your night in jail made up a unified act of self-satisfied principle. America might still own slaves and knuckle under to government, you at least had shown yourself free and could therefore go berrying. It was also an act of desperation, chosen because political circumstances had not yet allowed him a more effective one.

Looking around him, Thoreau found people who knew that slavery was wrong but would do nothing about it. As men they opposed it, as merchants or farmers they needed the protection of the government that supported it. Thoreau's understanding of the relation between principle and self-interest stemmed from the hardheaded late eighteenth century. When the two clashed, he knew that most would choose the pocketbook. The self-interest of millions stood behind the tax-collector. But the man of principle had no countervailing millions and had to choose a form of protest that could get along without them.

Even in 1846, however, Thoreau looked forward to a time when principle and self-interest would point the same way. If the just men were multiplied a thousand-fold and if each refused to work for the state or pay it or cooperate with it, then they might carry out a peaceful revolution. And if justice supported by multitudes could not win in peace, there was always the recourse of uprising and violence.

Four years later came the Fugitive Slave Law. The Massachusetts abolitionists organized a vigilance committee to protect Negroes who had escaped to freedom. Men banded together to rescue runaways who had been retaken by police and slavecatchers. When Anthony Burns was being legally deprived of his hard-won liberty, Thomas Higginson led an attack on the courthouse and almost set him free. In the too-little noticed speech called "Slavery in Massachusetts," Thoreau spoke out for Higginson and for all others who acted thus for freedom while the government acted for slavery.

He wasn't alone any longer. The official government represented by policemen and judges was being opposed by an unofficial government represented by the militant abolitionists. Higginson's support did not come from men who had divested themselves of self-interest by moving to a Walden Pond or a Fruitlands. Thoreau and Alcott had long ago returned from their broken utopias. His support was the same men and women who eight years earlier had been choosing the pocketbook. Thoreau discovered that the Massachusetts farmers and small-towners were beginning to find it expedient to act from principle.

He did not phrase it that way. Living much later, we can do so. There had always been a few ethical pioneers in the white community who knew slavery to be evil and knew it so deeply that they acted for freedom no matter what it cost them. But hatred of slavery became a political force only as merchants and industrialists and farmers and wage-earners learned that the planter-controlled government not only kept the Negro from freedom but stood between each of them and his own kind of freedom. When it became necessary to free the slaves in order to be free to pursue your own self-interest, principle and expediency fused, and then the Southern insurrection could be put down.

Just such a fusion marks today's campaign against segregation. When has the Negro not believed in equality? But only in the last half-dozen years has this beautiful idea voiced itself in a winning strategy. The economic advance that sent so many young people into the colleges did not put on individualist flannel. It had the examples of Africa and Asia, and it had leaders with the genius to borrow from abroad only what was already alive at home. The gathering whose symbol is Martin Luther King shows us justice supported by multitudes, testing our society to discover just how much equality can be won in peace. It takes exception to Thoreau's capacity for uprising, but looks back to him as the original American spokesman for massive non-violence.

Not so our campaign to prevent war, whose texture is still too thick with emotion and too bare of economics. Perhaps it is odd to say that your countrymen seem to have no self-interest in peace. But the workingman ogles the war contract as hungrily as his boss. Exporters of goods and money still try to sink their rivals in the common pool. No group finds it imperative to believe that its prosperity is impossible without disarmament. The campaign for peace is therefore led by the ethical pioneers, whose strategy is reminiscent of the come-outer and perfectionist in Henry Thoreau. They look back to "Civil Disobedience" for the courage it can always transmit to the isolated man of principle.

I have left something out. In Detroit there are hints of something new. A few Negro women have marched downtown with homemade signs against both war and segregation. A few white and Negro union officers have spoken at peace meetings and gotten together for serious study of anti-deterrent avenues. An occasional pacifist has begun to talk of non-violent resistance as a strategy for many rather than a way of life for a few. Detroit is not exceptional. Is it very surprising that the successors to McCarthy are concentrated in the South? The man most against equality turns out to be the man most for war and most against organized labor. When his opposites find it equally advantageous to join hands, the great moral issues of our day will fuse.

We shall still be reading "Civil Disobedience" then, for its spirit rather than its practicalities. Thoreau's is not a voice to be stilled. Listen to it: "All men recognize the right of revolution; that is, the right to refuse allegiance to, and to resist, the government, when its tyranny or its inefficiency are great and unendurable. But almost all say that such is not the case now. But such was the case, they think, in the Revolution of '75. If one were to tell me that this was a bad government because it taxed certain foreign commodities brought to its ports, it is most probable that I should not make an ado about it, for I can do without them. All machines have their friction; and possibly this does enough good to counterbalance the evil. At any rate, it is a great evil to make a stir about it. But when the friction comes to have its machine, and oppression and robbery are organized, I say, let us not have such a machine any longer. In other words, when a sixth of the population of a nation which has undertaken to be the refuge of liberty are slaves, and a whole country is unjustly overrun and conquered by a foreign army, and subjected to military law, I think that it is not too soon for honest men to rebel and revolutionize."

# FIVE WAYS OF LOOKING AT WALDEN

## WALTER HARDING

ALTHOUGH *Walden* was not exactly a roaring success when it was published in 1854—it took five years to sell out the first edition of only two thousand copies—it has become, in the century since, one of the all-time best sellers of American literature. It has been issued in more than one hundred and fifty different editions—with a number of these editions having sold more than half a million copies each. At this moment it is in print in at least twenty-four different editions in this country alone as well as in English language editions in England, India, and Japan and in translations into French, Spanish, Portuguese, Italian, German, Dutch, Norwegian, Finnish, Swedish, Danish, Czechoslovakian, Japanese, and Sanskrit. What are the causes of this phenomenal popularity?

For the past twenty-one years I have had the good fortune to be the secretary of the Thoreau Society—one of the most unpredictable groups of individualists that has ever united itself around a common enthusiasm. It is the only literary society I know of where the professional teachers of literature are vastly outnumbered by the non-professionals. Among the regular attenders of our annual meetings are a stockbroker, a retired letter carrier, a clergyman, an outspoken atheist, an entomologist, an ornithologist, a music teacher, an archeologist, a poet, a publishing company executive, a printer, a druggist, a socialist organizer, a hardware store owner, a church organist, the author of a book entitled *Why Work?* (each year he gets permission from the local police to sleep on the front porch of the Concord High School), a telephone company executive, a novelist, a conservationist, an exponent of subsistence farming, a woman who announces that she "covers the culture front in Brooklyn," a professional mountain climber, a crime expert—the list could go on almost indefinitely. What is even more interesting is that when these people have been asked to state why they are sufficiently interested in Thoreau to make the annual journey to Concord—and some of our most regular attenders come from as far away as Quebec, Illinois, North Carolina, and Texas—it is very rarely that two give the same reason. They are interested in his natural history, his politics, his economics, his prose style, his anarchism, his theology, and so on. The most phenomenal facet of Thoreau's appeal—and the appeal of his masterpiece, *Walden*—is its tremendous breadth. *Walden* is read, not for just one reason, but for many.

To most people, I suppose, *Walden* is a nature book. Certainly back at the time of its appearance it was almost universally considered to be a book about natural history, and some of Thoreau's contemporaries were annoyed that he allowed anything but nature to have a part in the book. The lengthy opening chapter on "Economy," they fussed, was a waste of time and should be skipped by the average reader. They also suggested the reader skip over such philosophical chapters as "Where I Lived and What I Lived For," "Higher Laws" and "Conclusion." When Thoreau wrote about ants or loons or muskrats or pickerel or squirrels or snow or ice, they argued, he was superb. But, unfortunately, he was all too ready to go off into transcendental nonsense comprehensible only to such "tedious archangels" as Amos Bronson Alcott or to such radical corrupters of idealistic American youth as Ralph Waldo Emerson. But on the birds, the bees, the flowers, and the weather Thoreau could write—and did write superbly. The late 19th Century anthologies of American literature, when Thoreau is included, almost invariably print "The Battle of the Ants" from the "Brute Neighbors" chapter of *Walden* or "The Pond in Winter."

I am not at all trying to belittle Thoreau as a nature writer. I am simply stating that that was his first and widest appeal—and in fact, still is. In the second-hand book stores of our country the dealers more often than not categorize him as a nature writer rather than as a literary figure or a philosopher.

It has been claimed—and I think quite rightfully—that he invented the natural history essay—and certainly his writings are the standard by which all nature writers since his time have been judged. He has successfully avoided the traps so many nature writers fall into of being too cute, too sentimental, too technical, or just plain dull. He never indulges in the pathetic fallacy of attributing human characteristics to the lower classes of animals. Yet neither does he write down to them. He accepts them for what they are and writes about them on their own terms. He writes about them with wit and humor—but the humor is as often at the expense of himself and his fellow man as at the expense of the animal. Take for example that passage near the end of his chapter on "Brute Neighbors" in which he talks about his checker game with the loon on Walden Pond:

> As I was paddling along the north shore one very calm October afternoon, for such days especially they settle on to the lakes, like the milkweed down, having looked in vain over the pond for a loon, suddenly one, sailing out from shore toward the middle a few rods in front of me, set up his wild laugh and betrayed himself. I pursued with a paddle and he dived again, but I miscalculated the direction he would take, and we were fifty rods apart when he came to the surface this time, for I had helped to widen the interval; and again he laughed long and loud,

and with more reason than before. He manoeuvered so cunningly that I could not get within half a dozen rods of him. Each time, when he came to the surface, turning his head this way and that he coolly surveyed the water and the land, and apparently chose his course so that he might come up where there was the widest expanse of water and at the greatest distance from the boat. It was surprising how quickly he made up his mind and put his resolve into execution. He led me at once to the widest part of the pond, and could not be driven from it. While he was thinking one thing in his brain, I was endeavoring to divine his thought in mine. It was a pretty game, played on the smooth surface of the pond, a man against a loon. Suddenly your adversary's checker disappears beneath the board, and the problem is to place yours nearest to where his will appear again. Sometimes he would come up un- expectedly on the opposite side of me, having apparently passed directly under the boat. . . . Once or twice I saw a ripple where he approached the surface, just put his head out to reconnoitre, and instantly dived again. I found that it was as well for me to rest on my oars and wait his reappearing as to endeavor to calculate where he would rise; for again and again, when I was straining my eyes over the surface one way, I would suddenly be startled by his unearthly laugh behind me. But why, after displaying so much cunning, did he invariably betray himself the moment he came up by that loud laugh? Did not his white breast enough betray him? He was indeed a silly loon, I thought. I could commonly hear the plash of the water when he came up, and so also detected him. But after an hour he seemed as fresh as ever, dived as willingly, and swam yet further than at first.

But so much for Thoreau as a nature writer.

A second appeal of *Walden* is as a do-it-yourself guide to the simple life. I think it highly significant that the first real surge of interest in Thoreau in the twentieth century came during the depres- sion years of the nineteen-thirties when large masses of people— indeed almost all of us—were required willy-nilly by the press of circumstances to adopt the simple life. We had no choice in the matter, but Thoreau was one of the very few authors who not only made this simple life bearable—he even made it appealing. A friend of mine said to me back in the thirties, "You know, Thoreau is the only author you can read without a nickel in your pocket and not be insulted."

What is perhaps more phenomenal than his appeal during the depression years is the fact that in our present era of super-materialism and status-seeking he still continues to make the simple life appealing. Now I am not one who advocates that we all, literally, go out and find our own Walden Ponds, build our own cabins, and ignore civilization. It was only through a profound misunderstanding of the book *Walden* that the idea that such an abandonment of civilization was Thoreau's aim ever got into circulation. He was very careful to say in the first chapter of *Walden:*

> I would not have any one adopt *my* mode of living on any account; for, beside that before he has fairly learned it I may have found out another for myself, I desire that there may be as many different persons in the world as possible; but I would have each one be very careful to find out and pursue *his own way,* and not his father's or his mother's or his neighbor's instead.

He himself lived at Walden only two of the forty-four years of his life—roughly about four per cent of his life. He went to Walden Pond to live because he had a specific purpose in mind—the writing of a book that he had found he did not have time to write if he spent his time keeping up with the proverbial Joneses. And when he had finished writing that book (incidentally that book was not *Walden* but its predecessor, *A Week on the Concord and Merrimack Rivers*), he left the pond as freely and as happily as he had gone there.

Thoreau's philosophy of the simple life does not advocate the abandonment of civilized life or a return to the jungle. He simply points out that modern life is so complex that it is impossible for each one of us to embrace all of it. We must of necessity be selective. But unfortunately our standards of selection tend to be imposed upon us by the society we live in rather than based on our own personal interests and desires. We live not our own lives but the lives imposed on us by those who surround us. We keep up with the Joneses instead of ourselves. And when we come to die, we discover that we have not lived. How many of us will be able to say as Thoreau did on his death-bed:

> I *suppose* that I have not many months to live; but, of course, I know nothing about it. I may add that I am enjoying existence as much as ever, and regret nothing.

"And regret nothing." Those are the key words. Are we able to say that honestly of our own lives? Thoreau, when he went to Walden Pond, said that he "wished to live deliberately, to front only the essential facts of life." And because he determined what was the essence of life—not for his parents, nor for his neighbors— but for himself, he was able to say at the end of his life that he regretted nothing.

How then does one get at the essence of life? All of *Walden* is devoted to answering that question. But perhaps we can find it epitomized in a brief quotation from his chapter entitled "Where I Lived and What I Lived For":

> Our life is frittered away by detail. An honest man has hardly need to count more than his ten fingers, or in extreme cases he may add his ten toes, and lump the rest. Simplicity, simplicity, simplicity! I say, let your affairs be as two or three, and not a hundred or a thousand; instead of a million count half a dozen, and keep your accounts on your thumb-nail. In the midst of this chopping sea of civilized life, such are the clouds and storms and quicksands and thousand-and-one items to be allowed for, that a man has to live, if he would not founder and go to the bottom and not make his port at all, by dead reckoning, and he must be a great calculator indeed who succeeds. Simplify, simplify. Instead of three meals a day, if it be necessary eat but one; instead of a hundred dishes, five; and reduce other things in proportion.
>
> Let us spend one day as deliberately as Nature, and not be thrown off the track by every nutshell and mosquito's wing that falls on the rails. Let us rise early and fast, or break fast, gently and without perturbation; let company come and let company go, let the bells ring and the children cry,—determined to make a day of it. . . . Why should we knock under and go with the stream? . . . Let us settle ourselves, and work and wedge our feet downward through the mud and slush of opinion, and prejudice, and tradition, and delusion, and appearance, that alluvion which covers the globe, through Paris and London, through New York and Boston and Concord, through Church and State, through poetry and philosophy and religion, till we come to a hard bottom and rocks in place, which we can call reality, and say, This is, and no mistake; and then begin, having a point d'appui, below freshet and frost and fire, a place where you might found a wall or a state, or set a lamp-post safely, or perhaps a gauge, not a Nilometer, but a Realometer, that future ages might know how deep a freshet of shams and appearances had gathered from time to time. . . . Be it life or death, we crave only reality. If we are really dying, let us hear the rattle in our throats and feel cold in the extremities; if we are alive, let us go about our business.

A third facet of *Walden* is its satirical criticism of modern life and living. Strangely enough this is one side of Thoreau that is

Walden Sat. July 5ᵗʰ '45

Yesterday I came here to live. My house makes me think of some mountain houses I have seen, which seemed to have a fresher auroral atmosphere about them as I fancy of the halls of Olympus. I lodged at the house of a saw-miller last summer, on the Caatskill mountains, high up as Pine Orchard in the blueberry & raspberry region, where the quiet and cleanliness & coolness seemed to be all one, which had their ambrosial character. He was the miller of the Kaaterskill Falls. They were a clean & wholesome family inside and out — like their house. The latter was not plastered — only lathed and the inner doors were not hung. The house seemed

Thoreau's Journal, July 5, 1845. *Reproduced with permission of the Trustees of The Pierpont Morgan Library.*

sometimes misunderstood by the reader. Some take everything Thoreau says literally and seriously, ignoring the fact that the book's epigraph reads:

> I do not propose to write an ode to dejection, but to brag as lustily as chanticleer in the morning, standing on his roost, if only to wake my neighbors up.

Even as astute a critic as James Russell Lowell made the rather astounding statement that Thoreau had no sense of humor. And if one does not see Thoreau's humor, he can be assured that he is missing—or worse, mis-reading a major portion of *Walden*.

A large portion of *Walden* cannot—or at least should not—be read literally. Thoreau had a rollicking, witty sense of humor and used it extensively throughout the pages of his masterpiece. He used just about every humorous literary device on record—puns, hyperbole, slapstick, mockery, parody, burlesque, and so on. And just about every one of these devices was used with satirical intent. It is true that now and then he gets off a pun just for the pun's sake—such as that worst—or best—of all puns in the chapter on "The Ponds" where he speaks of the patient but unlucky fishermen at Walden Pond being members of the ancient sect of "Coenobites." (At least one scholarly edition of *Walden* points out in a footnote that a Coenobite is "a member of a religious community," and ignores the pun about the fishermen—"See, no bites.") But such pure puns—if I may call them "pure"—are comparatively rare. Most of Thoreau's humor, as I have said, is directed at the foibles of contemporary society—and is not only directed at them, but hits with a wallop.

Unfortunately humor is almost impossible to demonstrate by excerpts. One of its essentials is that it be seen in context, for it is often its very context that makes it humorous. But let me try a few samples:

> The head monkey at Paris puts on a traveller's cap, and all the monkeys in American do the same.

> One farmer says to me, "You cannot live on vegetable food solely, for it furnishes nothing to make bones with"; and so he religiously devotes a part of his day to supplying his system with the raw material of bones; walking all the while he talks behind his oxen, which, with vegetable-made bones, jerk him and his lumbering plow along in spite of every obstacle.

> I observed that the vitals of the village were the grocery, the bar-room, the post-office, and the bank; and, as a necessary part of the machinery, they kept a bell, a big gun, and a fire-engine, at convenient places; and the

houses were so arranged as to make the most of mankind, in lanes and fronting one another, so that every traveller had to run the gauntlet, and every man, woman, and child might get a lick at him. Of course, those who were stationed nearest to the head of the line, where they could most see and be seen, and have the first blow at him, paid the highest prices for their places; and the few straggling inhabitants in the outskirts, where long gaps in the line began to occur, and the traveller could get over walls or turn aside into cow-paths, and so escape, paid a very slight ground or window tax.

If I should only give a few pulls at the parish bell-rope, as for a fire, that is, without setting the bell, there is hardly a man on his farm in the outskirts of Concord, notwithstanding that press of engagements which was his excuse so many times this morning, nor a boy, nor a woman, I might almost say, but would forsake all and follow that sound, not mainly to save property from the flames, but, if we will confess the truth, much more to see it burn.

We are eager to tunnel under the Atlantic and bring the Old World some weeks nearer to the New; but perchance the first news that will leak through into the broad, flapping American ear will be that the Princess Adelaide has the whooping cough.

If excerpting humor is dangerous, analyzing humor is even more so. Humor should stand on its own two legs—or it will fall flat on its face. But I wish to point out once again that Thoreau's humor is not used for its own sake. It is satirical humor and aimed at the reform of existing institutions and customs that Thoreau feels need the reform. And although we laugh at it—or with it—down deep underneath we realize there is often more validity to Thoreau's suggested reforms than to the customs of the society in which we live.

A fourth approach to *Walden* is the belletristic. From a purely technical standpoint, *Walden* is good writing and is worth examining as such. It has been frequently—and quite rightfully—said that Thoreau wrote the first modern American prose. One has only to compare a passage from *Walden* with one from almost any one of its contemporaries to see the difference. It was the vogue at the time to be abstract, circumlocutory, periphrastic, euphemistic, and euphuistic. *Walden* in contrast is clear, concrete, precise, and to the point. Emerson made the point a century ago when he said:

In reading Henry Thoreau's journal [and the same can be said of *Walden*], I am very sensible of the vigour of his constitution. That oaken strength which I noted whenever he walked, or worked, or surveyed wood-lots, the same unhesitating hand with which a field-labourer accosts a piece of work, which I should shun as a waste of strength, Henry shows in his literary task. He has muscle, and ventures on and performs feats which I am forced to decline. In reading him, I find the same thought, the same spirit that is in me, but he takes a step beyond, and illustrates by excellent images that which I should have conveyed in a sleepy generality. 'Tis as if I went into a gymnasium, and saw youths leap, climb, and swing with a force unapproachable,—though their feats are only continuations of my initial grapplings and jumps.

*Walden,* like Thoreau's cabin, is tightly constructed. Each sentence, each paragraph, and each chapter is in its carefully chosen niche and cannot be moved or removed without severe damage to the artistry of the whole. The basic unifying device of the book is the year. Although Thoreau spent two years, two months, and two days at Walden Pond, in writing the book he compressed his adventures into the cycle of one year. *Walden* opens with the cutting down of the pine trees in March and the construction of the cabin through the spring. In summer he moves into the cabin and tends his beanfield. In the autumn he builds his fireplace and warms his house. In the winter he observes his neighbors—human, animal, and inanimate. Then with the breaking up of the ice on the pond and the renascence of spring he brings his book to a close. One of the most interesting facets of Lyndon Shanley's *The Making of Walden* is his revelation of how carefully Thoreau reworked and transposed his sentences to better carry out this theme of the cycle of the year.

Each individual chapter in the book has its set place in the book as a whole. There is a careful alternation of the spiritual and the mundane ("Higher Laws" is followed by "Brute Neighbors"), the practical and the philosophical ("Economy" is followed by "Where I Lived and What I Lived For"), the human and the animal ("Winter Visitors" is followed by "Winter Animals"). Adjacent chapters are tied together by contrast (as "Solitude" and "Visitors"), by chronology (as "The Pond in Winter" and "Spring"), or by carefully worded connective phrases (as after "Reading" he begins "Sounds" with: "But while we are confined to books . . ." Or after "The Bean-Field" he begins "The Village" with: "After hoeing . . ."). And the three major expository chapters ("Economy," "Higher Laws," and "Conclusion") are placed strategically at the beginning, middle, and end of the book.

Within the individual chapters the details of construction are just as carefully worked out. In "The Ponds" he starts with Walden and then takes a southwestern sweep (his favorite direction for hiking according to his essay on "Walking") across Concord from Flint's Pond to Goose Pond to Fairhaven Bay, to White Pond. In "Former Inhabitants; and Winter Visitors," he starts with the residents of the days of the Revolution, works up through the most recent resident of the area—Hugh Quoil, who died the first autumn Thoreau was at the pond—and ends with those who visited him throughout his stay at the pond. Similar patterns can be worked out for each chapter.

Carefulness of construction continues into the individual paragraph. Although the average reader is not usually aware of it, Thoreau's paragraphs are unusually long. Walden contains only 423 paragraphs, an average of only slightly more than one page in the typical edition. But so carefully developed are they that one does not ordinarily notice their length. Their structure is so varied that there is little point in attempting to pick out typical examples. However, one of his favorite devices is at least worth mentioning— his use of the climax ending. Notice how frequently the final sentence in his paragraphs not only neatly sums up the paragraph as a whole, but usually carries it one step beyond, with an added thrust if the paragraph is satirical, with a broader concept if the paragraph is philosophical. Just as with his chapters, many of Thoreau's paragraphs are independent essays in themselves and can stand alone. But they cannot be moved from their specific niche within the book as a whole without damage to its structure.

Thoreau's sentences too are often unusually long. It takes very little search to find one half a page in length and more than one runs on for a full page and more. But again so carefully constructed are they that the average reader has no difficulty with their syntax and is hardly aware of their complexity. Let me take just one serpentine example from "House-Warming":

> I sometimes dream of a larger and more populous house, standing in a golden age, of enduring materials, and without gingerbread work, which shall still consist of only one room, a vast, rude, substantial, primitive hall, without ceiling or plastering, with bare rafters and purlins supporting a sort of lower heaven over one's head,—useful to keep off rain and snow, where the king and queen posts stand out to receive your homage, when you have done reverence to the prostrate Saturn of an older dynasty on stepping over the sill; a cavernous house, wherein you must reach up a torch upon a pole to see the roof; where some may live in the fireplace, some in the recess of a window, and some on settles, some at one end of the hall, some at another, and some aloft on rafters with the spiders, if they choose; a house which you have got into

when you have opened the outside door, and the ceremony is over; where the weary traveler may wash, and
eat, and converse, and sleep, without further journey; such
a shelter as you would be glad to reach in a tempestuous
night, containing all the essentials of a house, and nothing
for housekeeping; where you can see all the treasures of
the house at one view, and everything hangs upon its peg
that a man should use; at once kitchen, pantry, parlor,
chamber, storehouse, and garret; where you can see so
necessary a thing as a barrel or a ladder, so convenient a
thing as a cupboard, and hear the pot boil, and pay your
respects to the fire that cooks your dinner, and the oven
that bakes your bread, and the necessary furniture and
utensils are the chief ornament where the washing is not
put out, nor the fire, nor the mistress, and perhaps you are
sometimes requested to move from off the trapdoor,
when the cook would descend into the cellar, and so learn
whether the ground is solid or hollow beneath without
stamping.

Three hundred and fifty-one words—and yet I doubt if any attentive student has any difficulty with its meaning. I do not, however, want to give the impression that all of Thoreau's sentences
are grammatical leviathans. There are sentences in *Walden* only
five words in length. One extreme is as frequent as the other and
the majority are of more moderate length. Thoreau understood
fully the necessity of variety in sentence structure and length. The
point is that he could handle the sentence well no matter what its
length.

Perhaps the most noticeable characteristic of Thoreau's word
choice is the size of his vocabulary. *Walden* is guaranteed to send
the conscientious student to the dictionary. In a random sampling
we find such words as *integument, umbrageous, deliquium, ali-
ment, fluviatile,* and *periplus.* Yet Thoreau cannot be termed
ostentatious in his word-usage. He simply searches for and uses the
best possible word for each situation.

A second characteristic is his allusiveness. On a typical page he
may echo a Biblical phrase, quote from a metaphysical poet, trans-
late a few words from an ancient classic, make an allusion to a
Greek god, cite an authority on early American history, and toss
in a metaphor from a Hindu "Bible." It is true that he is usually
careful to make his allusions in such a way that knowledge of the
work alluded to is not essential to an understanding of Thoreau's
meaning. But the serious reader has his curiosity aroused and
wants his questions answered. To satisfy my own curiosity I once
took a list of more than fifty different types of figures of speech—
allusions, metaphors, rhetorical questions, alliteration, analogy,

puns, epanorthosis, parables, similes, meiosis, anti-strophe, oxy-moron, epizeuxis, anaphora, litotes, anti-thesis, portmanteau words, metonomy, contrast, personification, epistrophe, synec-doche, irony, apostrophe, hyperbole, and so on—and with no difficulty at all found excellent examples of each one in *Walden*. There is hardly a trick of the trade that Thoreau does not make use of. I think it significant that one of the most recent editions of *Walden*—one in fact published just this past year—is aimed for use as a textbook in college classes in rhetoric and grammar.

A fifth level on which to read *Walden* is the spiritual level. And I would not be exaggerating in the least to say that *Walden* has become veritably a bible—a guidebook to the higher life—for many, many people. In his chapter on "Reading," Thoreau says, "How many a man has dated a new era in his life from the reading of a book!" And *Walden* has been just such a book for many people. I spoke earlier of the fact that many of Thoreau's con-temporaries went out of their way to skip over such chapters as "Economy," "Where I Lived, and What I Lived For," "Higher Laws," and "Conclusion." Ironically it is just those chapters which are most essential to *Walden* as a spiritual guidebook. And it is interesting to note that our contemporary anthologies of American literature are tending to print excerpts from those chapters rather than from the natural history chapters that I spoke of earlier.

It is a major thesis of *Walden* that the time has come for a spiritual rebirth—a renewal and rededication of our lives to higher things. It is true that we have progressed a long way from the status of the caveman. But our progress has been for the most part material rather than spiritual. We have improved our means, but not our ends. We can unquestionably travel faster than our an-cestors, but we continue to waste our time in trivial pursuits when we get there. We have cut down on the number of hours of labor required to keep ourselves alive, but we have not learned what to do with the time thus saved. We devote the major part of our na-tional energy to devising new means of blowing up the rest of the world and ignore attempts to make better men of ourselves.

Thoreau could hardly be called orthodox from a religious stand-point (or, as a matter of fact, from any standpoint at all), but it is significant to note that one of his favorite texts was "What shall it profit a man if he gain the whole world but lose his own soul?" And *Walden,* on its highest level is a guide to the saving of your own soul, to a spiritual rebirth.

As many recent critics, from F. O. Matthiessen onward, have pointed out, the most frequently recurring symbol in *Walden* from the beginning of the book to the very end is the symbol of rebirth and renewal. The book as a whole, as I have said, is based on the cycle of the seasons ending with the renewal of the earth and its life with the coming of spring. The chapter on "Sounds" follows the same pattern for the day, beginning with the sounds of morning, continuing on through the afternoon, the evening, and the night, and ending with the renewal of the world from its sleep with the crowing of the cock in the morning. Thoreau speaks of the purification ceremonies of the Indians and of the Mexicans. He tells us of the strange and wonderful insect that was reborn out of the apple-tree table after sixty years of dormancy. The very closing words of the book are a promise of a newer and better life that can be achieved if we but strive for it:

> I do not say that John or Jonathan will realize all this; but such is the character of that morrow which mere lapse of time can never make to dawn. The light which puts out our eyes is darkness to us. Only that day dawns to which we are awake. There is more day to dawn. The sun is but a morning star.

How can we approach, how can we achieve such a life? We will find one answer in "Higher Laws":

> If one listens to the faintest but constant suggestions of his genius, which are certainly true, he sees not to what extremes, or even insanity, it may lead him; and yet that way, as he grows more resolute and faithful, his road lies. The faintest assured objection which one healthy man feels will at length prevail over the arguments and customs of mankind. No man ever followed his genius till it misled him. Though the result were bodily weakness, yet perhaps no one can say that the consequences are to be regretted, for these were a life in conformity to higher principles. If the day and the night are such that you greet them with joy, and life emits a fragrance like flowers and sweet-scented herbs, is more elastic, more starry, more immortal,—that is your success. All nature is your congratulation, and you have cause momentarily to bless yourself.

And the second is from his "Conclusion":

> I learned this, at least, by my experiment: that if one advances confidently in the direction of his dreams, and endeavors to live the life which he has imagined, he will meet with a success unexpected in common hours. He will put some things behind, will pass an invisible boundary; new, universal, and more liberal laws will begin to establish themselves around and within him; or the old laws be expanded, and interpreted in his favor in a more liberal sense, and he will live with the license of a higher order of beings. In proportion as he simplifies his life, the

laws of the universe will appear less complex, and solitude will not be solitude, nor poverty poverty, nor weakness weakness. If you have built castles in the air, your work need not be lost; that is where they should be. Now put the foundations under them.

Thoreau is sometimes dismissed as a misanthrope or a skulker, one who devoted himself to carping and criticism. But note that when *Walden* is approached on this spiritual level, it is not negative, it is positive. Thoreau is not so much complaining about the way things are but rather showing the way things might be. He is firmly convinced that the sun *is* but a morning star.

I have approached *Walden* from five different angles. But I have by no means exhausted the number of such approaches. *Walden* can and does mean all things to all men. Therein lies its very strength. It has been tested by time and not found wanting. In its first hundred years it has grown, not diminished in stature. I have no fear as to its being lost sight of in one more century—or two—or three—or four. It will endure.

# FANNY ECKSTORM'S BIAS

## MARY P. SHERWOOD

SEVERAL COMMENTS have long been needed by a trained naturalist on Fanny Eckstorm's criticism, "Thoreau's 'Maine Woods,'" which appeared in the *Atlantic Monthly* for July, 1908. Mrs. Eckstorm was unusually qualified for making such a criticism, but her approach to discussing Thoreau as an outdoorsman was greatly warped. She was so enamored with the state of Maine that she resented anything coming in from the outside, especially if tainted with any suggestion of superiority over her forest darlings. Also, most unscientifically for a person with a mind otherwise demanding accuracy, she was at times prone to form an opinion first and test the accuracy of it afterwards.

While Mrs. Eckstorm starts out with statements which indicate she is commenting on critics of Thoreau, most of whom depended upon Emerson's eulogy, she gives the over-all impression that she is criticizing Thoreau directly. This leads readers not trained in natural history to feel that Henry was but a lower echelon boy scout after all. Had Henry Thoreau been born in Maine Mrs. Eckstorm's pen would likely have celebrated her possession of him. But leaning so heavily in a negative direction, she needs setting into truer line with more substantial facts.

Quotes Fanny from Emerson: ". . . he could pace 16 rods more accurately than another man could measure them with rod and chain." She adds, "That is nonsense, for it puts at naught the whole science of surveying." How right she makes her comment sound.

It is customary for forest surveyors to become proficient at pacing off relatively short distances, for it isn't always convenient to drag a chain around. Long, tedious practice goes into establishing a conditioned pacing stride, usually of three feet, for measuring along ground surface. A fifty-foot line is marked off and the trainee paces over and over it until his legs develop an automatic feel of the three-foot step, often taking months to attain perfection.

Foresters use pacing, for instance, when making height measurements of trees with use of a hand level; it would be impractical to measure out the distance with a chain from every tree. Pacing is used by all surveyors, since even the measurement of bounds seldom requires accuracy to the inch. Thoreau had trained himself to pace with dependable accuracy. On February 3, 1860, he recorded in his Journal: "I accurately pace the swamp in two directions and find it shaped thus:—" On the following page is a rough map which he titled, "Gowing's Swamp. (Scale of forty paces to an inch)." No doubt Emerson had seen him at his pacing on many occasions and had ample opportunity to check Henry's figures with a rule or chain.

Mrs. Eckstorm also misses, deliberately or otherwise, Emerson's meaning of the words, "more accurately than *another man* could measure with rod and chain." The italics are mine but no doubt those two words were limned in Emerson's mind. Using a rod and chain is supposed to be the more accurate way of measuring than pacing, but in the hands of a careless or less particular man than Thoreau, measuring tools can be used sloppily. In Thoreau's hands a rod and chain were precision instruments; surveyors who have gone over his maps in recent years have pronounced him a dependable worker whom it is almost impossible to improve upon even with more modern instruments.

Emerson said, "He could find his path in the woods at night better by his feet than by his eyes." Mrs. Eckstorm says that this "Is nothing remarkable. . . . How does one keep the path across his own lawn on a black night?"

You cross your own lawn in the dark by responding to conscious learned knowledge and to conditioned reflexes. You know approximately where everything is. Automatically and deliberately you line up all objects in their proper perspective, and your feet, unless covered with very heavy soles, can feel the unencumbered path.

Finding the path in the woods at night is quite different since you usually don't know every tree, rock or other object. Here you also rely on learned information, and the broader your woods knowledge the easier it is, but it is *not* as simple as walking on your lawn path. The soil of a woods path is packed much more solidly than the humus soil along both sides. Also, the path is much clearer of sticks, rocks and general forest debris, and if it is used much there are no seedlings to stub your toes or brush against your legs, except along the path edges. An experienced woods walker knows almost instantly when he steps off the path in the dark, for suddenly the soil is springier, there is ground surface debris, and things are brushing against his legs. If it is a black night it might be necessary to walk slowly to keep to the path, bringing all the senses to bear upon the situation. This is relatively easy to learn, if you know woods lore; but Fanny is wrong when she implies anyone can do it. Most people can't for the simple reason that few have trained their senses to that extent.

I have a suspicion that Fanny did not have this skill, hence her lack of understanding of what it involves; nor did her Penobscot woodsmen have it for the reason that no such worn paths existed in their woods, and surely they couldn't find their boot-nail tracks in the boulder-strewn black spruce woods at night. Maine woodsmen found their way around their camps at night by the light of huge fires, and usually they wore such hulking boots they couldn't have felt a path with their feet if there had been one.

Mrs. Eckstorm's removal of the word "path" from Emerson's sentence is too obviously an attempt to look for something to quibble about. Any writer can remove the key word from anybody's sentence and change the whole intent.

As to Thoreau's ability to measure distances and speeds, it was inevitable that Mrs. Eckstorm would feel she needed to defend her Indians who couldn't apply the white man's time, distance and speed measurements. But she juggles words when she says, "No Penobscot boatman can run a batteau over falls at the rate of 15 miles per hour." There is a vast difference between running a boat over falls, and running it down rapids. What Henry said was, "In shooting the rapids . . . the boatman . . . is moving steadily on at the rate of fifteen miles per hour." Two pages further on he adds, "Here was the longest rapid in our voyage. . . . Shooting down sometimes at the rate, we judged, of fifteen miles per hour. . . ." Notice the "we." It included McCauslin and Fowler, called two of the best boatmen on the Penobscot. No doubt they were the ones who determined this figure, and Henry's self-set task was to report what he saw and heard along the way.

As to Fanny's argument that it was impossible for a batteau to travel a hundred miles in a day, how long a day was she or Henry speaking of? How loaded the boat, how many men to row and pole? Was a sail used on the lakes, since the Indians often used a blanket for a sprit-sail; was the wind in the right direction, and how much of such a trip was downstream? With conditions in the boatmen's favor, using all navigational aids possible and traveling over fast rapids with a minimum of portages, maybe such speed was consistently possible. But if Henry said that a hundred miles was a good average day's speed then someone else told him that, either McCauslin, Fowler, the Indians, or someone in the stagecoach or at Old Town, since his party never covered that much ground in one day. Henry was forever asking questions and incorporating the answers in his notes. But we must notice that nowhere in her article does Fanny suggest that her woodsmen might have given Henry false information now and then.

Where Thoreau states that his surveyor's eye could detect a slope to the waterways in three different places, Fanny says that any woman who can tell when a picture hangs straight on a wall could see those slopes, that Henry belittles his surveyor's skill. I say that Fanny never took many girls or women camping or on field trips. She could see the slopes because her father trained her to see such things when she was a child. Most of the people I know would never be aware of a slight inclined ground-level plane against the level planes of surrounding rock structures. The only seeing eye is the trained eye.

Thoreau's worst error in judgment, says Mrs. Eckstorm, "is the error he made in climbing Katahdin." Here she is guilty of many things, including hindsight. She blithely adds, "Instead of climbing by the Slide, where all West Branch parties ascend today, he laid a northeast course directly for the base of the highest peak, through all the debris and underbrush at the foot of the mountain. . . ." She says his camp was not five miles in an air-line from the top of the South Slide.

Very few people were known to have climbed Katahdin before Henry arrived there, and not until later did he learn that some of them used the Slide. He reports seeing the Slide, but knowing nothing about it he apparently considered it a dangerous route for his party. McCauslin and Fowler were with him, but they had never been further in than the river.

We must remember that Henry was at Katahdin to see and learn all he could about it in a very short time. It was essential for him to poke into glens, to look over the talus slope, to see the rock formations around the mountain's sides, to get the lay of the boulders in the area, and to determine what plants were there. By leading his party the long way around he saw and learned far more for his writings and his talks than he ever could have in the shorter five miles up the bare rock Slide.

Mrs. Eckstorm conveniently passed over one sentence which could have had considerable bearing on his choice of route. Henry wrote, "At length, fearing that if we held the direct course to the summit, we could not find any water near our camping-ground, we gradually swerved to the west. . . ." A perfectly logical and sensible reason for taking a longer way around in strange country where they planned to camp out overnight.

This brings us to the much maligned bird list, which writers are pouncing upon today with Fanny's help. Although Thoreau was not as good an ornithologist as he was a student of other aspects of nature, Fanny's comments are tinged with the scorn of one who possesses hindsight and who fancies she has an axe to grind. By the time she wrote her article, Chapman's *Handbook of the Birds of Eastern North America* had been on the market eight years, and other taxonomies and bird life histories were in print. None of these books was available to Thoreau. He did use Gray's *Manual,* printed in 1847, for his report on plants, which indicates he would have probably used a bird manual had one existed.

Bird watching is always a challenge because of the mobility of birds and the great variations of plumage, the latter including courtship colors, confusing fall plumages, eclipse colors of some species, and the subdued immature and female plumages. Light conditions can trip the best field identifiers. Serious list-keeping is impossible without a good pair of binoculars in one hand and an official field identification book in the other. Henry Thoreau had all the frustrations to contend with and none of the tools; his little monocular spy glass was close to useless.

There is, however, a curious lack of enthusiasm throughout Thoreau's writings for the bird inhabitants of his beloved fields and woods. This is especially noticeable when you consider his intense attention to sound; surely nothing in nature produces more remarkable sound than birds. I have often felt that Henry just stood on the sidelines, only secretively listening, as if deliberately leaving the bird world to his lost, bird-loving brother John.

Whatever the reason, it doesn't mean that Henry Thoreau was incapable of learning as much about birds as anyone else in his time, and more. We must remember that one of his chosen limitations was never to kill birds or collect skins other than the few skins he turned over to Louis Agassiz. In his day it was essential to have a bird in the hand for positive identification. Even today a professional ornithologist won't accept a field record about which there can be the slightest doubt unless he has the bird or the skin at hand. Only a handful of people in all United States history have attained such skill at field identification of birds that their sight records go unquestioned. No present-day ornithologist accepts the lists of Thoreau's time without ferreting out all the information possible and checking all known collections from the area. Thus to question Thoreau's list is not to make him out to be a poor bird watcher.

The advanced modern bird watcher has years of specialized college training behind him; he has excellent binoculars and telescopes, countless authoritative books, and the new sound recording equipment, including the spectrograph. A few who possess all this visual and sound aid equipment are using Eckstorm's article as a jump-off to ridicule Thoreau's skill, in turn strengthening the Eckstorm criticism, which becomes criticism in its most unfair form.

Although there are some errors in Thoreau's *Maine Woods* list, they are not as bad as Fanny makes them out to be. Perhaps the redheaded woodpecker is the biggest snag; it could only have been the pileated since the redhead has just recently extended its range into New England, but at least it was a woodpecker and it did have a red head. Was the lighting so poor Henry caught but a glimpse of the bird in those dark woods? Joe Polis must have known which species it was, for he was the one, not Henry, as Fanny implies, who commented it was good to eat. Surely, crowded in that little birch canoe, Joe heard Henry call it a redheaded woodpecker; why didn't Joe correct him? Could it be that Polis didn't know there was another woodpecker elsewhere, with a red head and much smaller? Has Fanny blown up a smoke screen to protect the Indian?

Mrs. Eckstorm smugly states, "Seven out of thirty-seven birds are too wrong to be disputed." This sounds far more derogatory than if she had said thirty of his thirty-seven birds were probably right. Certainly he was correct with the overwhelming majority.

Then she adds a sentence which distorts the thinking of any reader who isn't an experienced bird watcher. She boldly says, "If we had fuller data of the forest regions, perhaps several of the others might be challenged." It is far more likely that, had we fuller data for that area of Maine in Thoreau's time, it might be found that more of Henry's species were present than less. We have learned in recent years that bird population displacement occurs, and contraction and expansion of ranges, for several reasons. By the time Thoreau got into Maine most of the vast white pine stands had been removed, which could have changed or initiated changes in the species present then. By the time Fanny wrote her article much of the spruce and other species had been cut for pulpwood, no doubt causing further bird population changes between Henry's time and hers. Thus records for either of those periods can't ever be considered accurate, for it requires many observers, taking notes and collecting skins over a definite area for a long period of time, to produce scientifically acceptable data.

Henry's mistake of calling the horned grebe a bufflehead is understandable, especially without binoculars in poor light. The young of the grebe, almost adult size by July, are grayish black and silvery white, and Henry says it was a family group he observed. The bufflehead is black and white, thus there is some similarity.

For Fanny to call Henry for not having the Canada jay on his list at the back of the book, the bird which she names as the most characteristic of the area, when he does describe it nicely in the text is again looking for something to criticize. Who edited or checked that list against the text? Sophia? Channing? Henry was dead by the time it went to a publisher. Did the printer accidentally leave the jay out? Also, probably Fanny wasn't aware that the opening up of the forest in her day brought in more jays than would have been found in the dense, darker woods of Henry's time.

We now come to that amazing statement of Mrs. Eckstorm's: "Of the scientific ardor which works without books and collates and classifies innumerable facts for the sake of systematic knowledge, he had not a particle." This is an indigestible sentence. In the first place, anyone with scientific ardor doesn't work without books. Even in Thoreau's time. Also, it is indisputable that Thoreau spent a large part of his life collecting innumerable facts, even "setting traps for them." That was what he was in Maine for.

His *Journals* and his voluminous Indian notebooks are primarily a record of his gathered-in facts, with many references to his collating them against or with other writers. He did try, even desperately, to arrive at some form of systematic knowledge and might have reached at least part of his goal had he lived another twenty years. Maybe Fanny confused her terms. By "systematic knowledge" she may have meant "systematic classification", but if so she tried to make of Henry what he refused to be—a taxonomist. In her very next sentence she admits his notes are voluminous, thus contradicting herself. And how could they have been voluminous without the ardor to make them so?

We can forgive her next words as times have changed since she wrote them, even though she should have anticipated some of the changes. Of Henry's innumerable notes, she says that though they are "of the greatest interest, [they] rarely furnish material for science." The modern student of Thoreau must not be tripped by that out-moded evaluation.

Quite the opposite is now true. Interminable digging has been done in Thoreau's mine of notes by scientists of many disciplines. Today he is considered the father of limnology for his detailed notes on stream and lake biology and physics. He is recognized as the first to work out plant succession through his study of pine trees—a concept which present day botanists, ecologists and wildlife managers could not do without. His botanical data are quoted in many modern classification and geographic range books; one of the first to use his information, even before his *Journals* were published, was the *Flora of Middlesex County, Massachusetts*. Meteorologists have found pay dirt in his *Journals* for they badly need dependable data of a hundred years and more ago in order to work out weather trends and cycles; few were the weather observers and note-takers in those days. Henry Thoreau is considered our first real ecologist, and he was also one of the first, if not the first, phenologist in the country. None of these sciences, except botany, was in existence then; he helped lay their foundations. He was such a meticulous worker that his notes have considerable value despite the fact that we now consider several machines and gadgets essential for accurate observation. In many cases his data are all that we have for his time, so we are fortunate in the quality of his work.

I can find no excuse for Mrs. Eckstorm, however, when she says, "It was not as an observer that Thoreau surpassed other men, but as an interpreter." What a strange sentence. How can anyone be an interpreter until he has first observed? To be a good interpreter one must be a good observer; Henry was both. He deliberately trained all of his senses to observe to the ultimate. He was an observer all of his adult life, else his twenty-volume works could never have come into existence.

Fanny relents a bit to express appreciation of Thoreau's philosophy, but she quickly spoils it with the startling statement, "Thoreau knew nothing of woodcraft." She then states that his longest trip in Maine gave him only ten days in the woods.

If she had said he knew nothing of *Maine* woodcraft she might have had a leg to stand on. But even so, the word "nothing" is unacceptable since he did lead the trip up Katahdin and back without mishap; more than once he found the opening of the river ahead before the Indians did; he heard the moose before Aitteon did, and he found his way to Chamberlain Lake over an obliterated trail. And Fanny ignored all that was known of his vast knowledge of Concord woodcraft.

Henry admitted being incapable of taking care of himself alone in the Maine woods, with its wolves and bears, its lack of natural food even in the streams, its vicious rapids and high falls and obscure passages along the rivers, and its long, bitter winter. The very fact that he was in Maine but three times, ten days at the longest and each time in an amenable season, meant that he wasn't familiar enough with Maine woods life. Give him a year's experience working with the loggers and river drivers, traveling with trappers and tree explorers, and he would have grasped all the knowledge he needed for living in the Maine woods. But Fanny was as aware as he that it wasn't wise for anyone to travel or live in that wilderness alone.

Still Thoreau could have shown either Polis or Fanny a thing or two on his own Concord ground.

Where Mrs. Eckstorm discusses the carry trail she says that in the spring a hundred men had trampled over that carry for days, wearing boots with 29 one-inch spikes in the soles of each. "The whole carry," she says, "had been pricked out like an embroidery pattern." What she doesn't add is that the growing season in northern Maine is very short, between the last spring frost and the first fall frost. Plants run through their life cycles in something of a hurry in order to mature seeds or spores before the fall killing frost. Mosses and ground vegetation become inches thick and lush in a few warm weeks of summer. By mid-July the ground is thickly carpeted with deep moss and other small plants. Pricks made by only one-inch-long spikes in spring would be mostly obliterated by then. That Polis could see any traces of the pattern was because of his familiarity with it. If Henry Thoreau had ever seen a carry at the height of the spring log drive, he too probably would have recognized remnants of the spike tracks. He did see them, of course, where they were obvious on the rocks.

Fanny gives the incident of Henry's leading his companion off

65

the carry onto the tote road as proof of his lack of woodcraft knowledge. Yet in the same breath she says, "He took the tote road, used only for winter hauling, showing neither hoof mark, sled track nor footprint in summer. . . ." Here too the trail was covered with thick moss, and she ignores the fact that he found his way over the obliterated trail. Henry had with him a compass and an old map; skill in using them is considered good woodcraft. But Fanny called him "only a pasture man."

Mrs. Eckstorm's contention that because Thoreau borrowed an axe to build his Walden hut he was no woodsman, since a woodsman always owns his own axe, is nonsense. The Thoreau family owned an axe, and it was needed at home where Henry did his share of splitting wood for the family. He needed an extra axe only long enough to clear the hut site; no doubt he used the family axe later to split his own wood. He was keeping deliberate record of his expenses; he had little cash to spend and wanted to keep the cost of the building to a minimum to make his point that only a small outlay was necessary to obtain shelter. It was a literary as well as a financial consideration. There was no real reason to have an extra axe; he wasn't a logger, it was not part of his job or philosophy to go around chopping down trees. The tools of his own trade he did have: paper, pens, pencils and a few books. Later, when he became a surveyor, he owned his surveying instruments. Not owning an axe while he was at Walden couldn't possibly have any bearing on Henry's woodcraft skill.

Fanny's Maine woodsmen engaged in at least three different types of forest craftsmanship, and Henry's way was another. That he was able to match wits with her men, and proved superior in some ways, was so obvious it stuck in Fanny's crop. This is what she felt compelled to disprove. In order to do so she let herself stoop to dissembling and to invention. Had Henry been Maine born she might have torn to shreds anyone who had written such nonsense about him.

After going to all her trouble to look for things to criticize she suddenly allows: "Because he made some mistakes in unimportant details, he must not be accused of being unreliable." If all her claims in that 1908 article were true, Henry David Thoreau would certainly have been an unreliable man.

But as Fanny says herself, "After the woods shall have passed away, the vision of them as he saw them will remain." Today Thoreau's *Maine Woods* appeals to the forester, the ecologist, the hunter, the adventurous canoeist and mountain climber. It was Henry Thoreau, the articulate woodsman, who created one of the most coniferous-pungent books in the English language, a book which a century later still remains one of the best written on the woods of Maine.

# WALDEN REVISITED

*THOMAS P. McDONNELL*

I read you, Thoreau, once too much
(Buddha ensconced in a concord sky)
I fished in the lake at Littleton—
The pickerel snapped the silken line.

Drizzle descended on the lily pads
(Out on the lake the slick loon laughed)
I pushed toward shore and there surprised
A porcupine in the juniper bush.

The beekeeper gave me tea to drink
*(Natives of the rain are rainy men)*
We talked of Plato and swatted fat flies—
The afternoon droned softly by.

The moon uprose and pushed the trees
Too high for birds in the nimbus nest—
When Henry played the Chinese flute
I fled to town and drank like death.

# CORN GROWS IN THE NIGHT

## THEODORE BAIRD

ANYONE WHO SITS DOWN TO READ straight through the *Bulletins* of the Thoreau Society—whose members collect and print every scrap of news about their author—is bound to notice how variously a literary man can be put to what are after all non-literary uses. Those expectations associated with Swift or Pope or Jane Austen, subtlety of thought and feeling and expression, the creation of a coherent imagined world to which we respond with pleasurable emotion, are subordinated to something large and vague called an influence, a political and social force, a public image, even a property worth dollars and cents. Like the Lincoln of the Lincoln Memorial or Dr. Schweitzer on the cover of *Time,* Thoreau now looms as an international figure. He seems to stand for private rebellion. He is the solitary man against society, appealing to the individual's profound dissatisfaction with the part he must play in earning a living, in just being a member of the human race. Furthermore Thoreau preaches a better life within walking distance: after a left turn you come to a woods and a pond. So it is that Thoreau has even been mentioned in the same breath with Jesus and with Gandhi.

No wonder, then, that a watchful eye finds Thoreau's name in so many odd connections that the *Bulletin* is able to publish in every issue a column of the latest news of their author, how he is put to use in Seattle, what new translation has been made in Spanish. Single sentences of his appear, we are told, on bus cards in such and such a city, and the curious fact is added that these cards are often stolen. He also provides quotations to be used, along with Elbert Hubbard, in the calendars of savings banks, and, along with John Locke, in the prestige advertising of great corporations. His name is invoked on behalf of good causes, as if there were something about him that would naturally make him a proponent of homeopathy and vegetarianism, of theosophy and phonetic spelling and organic gardening. He has been acknowledged as their model by a number of people who have taken to the woods and tried living on woodchuck and purslane or soybeans, and Paul Elmer More in Shelburne, N. H. complacently wrote *A Hermit's Notes on Thoreau* and actually professed to have read *Walden* out of doors. Thoreau has also been loosely associated with nature as a picture, especially when charmingly recorded by the camera, and it seemed as proper in 1906 to adorn the edition of the *Journal* with a series of fine illustrations—snow on pitch pines, a wildflower—as it did more recently for *Life* to run what is called a photographic essay on Thoreau. Appropriately, as a piece of property Thoreau's money value does not seem great. Of course the Morgan and Huntington Libraries do possess manuscripts. And why not? But a pencil made by Thoreau, an empty pencil box, a couple of bricks from his birthplace, are modestly priced, and an ordinary first edition of *Walden,* while more expensive than a Chauncey Depew item, may cost less than a good Currier and Ives.

Such relations as these are scarcely literary. Of course Thoreau does have his earnest readers, and some of them make the most extraordinary claims for their author, as an "influence," as an instrument useful in locating the good life. Some such assertions have been made, for example, by Upton Sinclair, Robert W. Service, John Buchan, Bette Davis, Bernard Baruch, Gypsy Rose Lee, Henry Miller. Thoreau has also had his solitary reader, the one-book man, puzzling and brooding over the text as if it were a religious document, finding in it a new confidence for trusting in his own incommunicable inner life. Then there are those for whom the essay on "Civil Disobedience" serves as the classic document for signing a separate peace treaty and resigning from society. It is seriously reported that every now and then someone deciding he will no longer pay his income tax sends a copy of this essay to the nearest Collector of Internal Revenue as an explanation, as an intelligible explanation. In other acts of defiance of constituted authority Thoreau is appealed to. The marchers against a missile base in Kansas are said to have named Thoreau as a writer who justified their conduct. So when Dr. Uphaus took a copy of "Civil Disobedience" with him to his New Hampshire jail he defined for anyone who knew anything his own position. Curiously it was as long ago as the 1890's that Thoreau served such purposes in Britain, and the textbooks tell us that he has had his effect on Gandhi and the Labour movement. As for the immediate disturbed present, when some token resistance is made at the launching of every submarine, when civil defense regulations are deliberately violated, when riders are on their way to New Orleans and walkers on their way to Moscow, when sitters occupy Whitehall, who can say where in the many aggressive acts of individual conscience Thoreau's name is not a living force? When we read as an item of biographical interest that Kenneth Kaunda has served a prison term in Northern Rhodesia for possessing books advocating non-violence, do we not think back with astonishment to that scene in Concord, Massachusetts, that ordinary scene in which no voices were raised, when Thoreau on his way to the cobbler's was arrested by Sam Staples, the night spent in jail, and the next day the huckleberrying as usual? "The air is filled with sounding boards and the echoes are flying," said John Jay Chapman, speaking in the purest Concord idiom. And so it would seem. Apparently Thoreau's voice does carry from continent to continent. He is heard by all sorts of people, as if he were shouting his most intimate thoughts across Walden Pond, and they know what he means. The separate words may be blurred, but distinct speech, we know, is only for the convenience of those who are hard of hearing.

In addition to the revolutionary, the rebellious, and the crack-pot, the English teacher has often made Thoreau into a special property, and again for reasons that can hardly be called literary. Thoreau has been blown up way out of proportion compared with, say, Emerson. He is presented, along with Dostoievski, as a treat for the bright high school student, and, along with Jacques Barzun, as a stimulating writer in the book of readings aimed at shaking loose the thick wits of college freshmen. In the classroom he is used to make quick and easy relations between literature and life. The teacher can begin by quoting this bit of English prose: " 'Pay . . . or be locked up.' I declined to pay." He can describe the night in jail—in all the history of human suffering, how it is remembered —and then allude to the many cells now or lately occupied by the many people, some of them almost children, who have sought arrest because their conscience demanded it. Then there can be quoted the words of the Federal judge—it is unlikely that they will ever be included in a volume of stimulating essays for freshmen— when sentencing for more than a single night, for as much as four years, some pacifists who tried to hinder the launching of a nuclear submarine: "While all of you may be sincerely desirous of moving the world in the direction of peace and goodwill, the court can-not accept your decision to accomplish this highminded end by means of breaking the Federal law." Other examples of organized protest are everywhere so common it is inconceivable that a class would not soon be arguing the rights and wrongs of everything. It may seem then that literature is at last, finally and unmistakably, connected with life, with things that matter.

When a writer is put to such diverse uses, as a thinker of great thoughts, as an example of desirable anti-social behavior, as an authority sanctioning the individual's reliance on his own judg-ment, as an encourager of organized protest, and, at the lowest level, as a bludgeon to rouse sluggish wits, you have evidence of something extravagant. The attention to Thoreau, and admiration for him, is out of all reasonable bounds. He is, in fact, the center of a cult. At its beginning Lowell protested, and to this day he has never been forgiven. Quite recently when Perry Miller in *Con-sciousness in Concord* demonstrated in a tone of excusable acri-mony that Thoreau has his limitations both as a man and as a writer, the reply was a scream of outrage. Perry Miller noticed that the more readers Thoreau has had "the more they try not to recognize his lineaments." The big nose, the weak chin, the high

Yankee style with its frequent tones of querulousness, the extremely self-conscious stylist fitting sentences together, in the comparison made by a contemporary, as if he were working in mosaic, all this is blurred, and as if they were listening to the humming of telegraph wires his readers fill in the words from their own highest yearnings and deepest dissatisfactions.

Nevertheless Thoreau's position as a writer can be located, and let the worst be said first of all. He is an impossible egotist. Why, wrote one of his oldest friends, was he so disappointed with everybody else &c., not even putting it in the form of a question and making the object all inclusive. Thoreau speaks as the exception to every rule, the judge of all the rest of the universe, droning on and on, monotonously didactic, deliberately obscure, about friendship and chastity and the soul and things like that, all the while playing with words, seeing similarities in differences, differences in similarities, punning and turning out paradoxes. No wonder Hawthorne called him an intolerable bore. But Thoreau's own awareness of where he stood in relation to his friends gives us some idea of the high visibility of the Concord air, so clear, dry, and cold it was. He actually says of himself, "My only distinction must be that I am the greatest bore they ever had."

And the portentous tone still comes through to us. Thus he says, for example, "Silence alone is worthy to be heard." The fact is that once you give your mind to this way of talking you can set yourself up as a sage, and with the same effect. Insensibility, one can say, alone is worthy of being felt . . . The invisible alone is worthy of being seen . . . The intangible alone we want to touch . . . The incommunicable . . . The ineffable . . . "Give me that sentence," says Thoreau, "which no intelligence can understand." Well? The question is answered by Thoreau again from his own terrible awareness of what he was doing. On the publication of *Walden* he wrote down in his *Journal* a list of his faults as a writer, and he begins with "Paradoxes . . . a style which may be imitated." Profundity turns out to be a surface obscurity, and that which no intelligence can understand a trick of style.

To continue the catalogue of faults, Thoreau also enjoys the easy position of the moralist. You can watch him walk into and establish the obvious connections. When he sees a sloop off Chatham dragging for anchors, he goes on in the entirely expected way: "If the roadsteads of the spiritual ocean could be thus dragged, what rusty flukes . . ." and so on and on, where the shift from the material to the spiritual meaning is explicit and traditional. The ocean of life. Throw out the lifeline. A great deal of Thoreau is like this, obvious, soothing, expected, on the level of hymn writing and the common cant of sermons.

Having said all this in obvious disparagement, I add that there is a lot of fun in Thoreau. It is too bad he did not preserve more bits of conversation with his Uncle Charles, more examples of human oddity, like that of the man who began to dig through to China. We have Emerson's word for it that his Concord audience —how experienced they were in listening to lecturers—laughed till they cried over his description of his rambles on Cape Cod, and there is a great deal of laughter still available on the printed page. Thoreau's humor is like that of another Yankee who sailing alone around the world repelled the attacks of hostile natives by strewing his deck with carpet tacks and so reduced their bloodthirstiness and his own real danger to something more than a little ludicrous. In his highest flights where Thoreau is at his best there is this same awareness of the fun of the thing, an awareness that he is playing the part of a sage, homespun, crackerbarrel, local, living right there along with the many other sages in Concord. He shows us how every American can be his own philosopher, and what a funny idea that is.

As a writer, however, Thoreau must be taken with the utmost seriousness. "Hardly in the history of literature, wherever we enter the workshop, is there such devotion to duty," says Perry Miller, and we can follow the author from one stage to another in the manufacture of the finished product. First there is the author out of doors, often—and this comes as a surprise—carrying an umbrella, sometimes accompanied by his unnamed friend (Channing) and his nameless dog (Peter). We can see him stopping to write in his notebook, recording frequently in the present tense a scene or object before his eyes. Later there was the writing up of these notes and then their revision in the *Journal*. Finally there was the ransacking of the *Journal*, the dovetailing and patching in book and essay, making that rich texture where every sentence and metaphor connect with a constantly enlarging complex of imagery and thought. Indeed it might even be said that part of Thoreau's present importance is a result of the rich material he offers the analytical reader.

Even more remarkable than the intricacy of his arrangements on the page is his extraordinary use of language to communicate the incommunicable, to express those wordless moments when Thoreau stood alone in the presence of his subject. And what, precisely, was that subject? Nature, we say, and everyone knows that nature for Thoreau was but a figure of speech. "—I use a part of the world as a symbol to express my thought," and nature, he says, provides the "raw material of tropes and symbols with which to describe . . . life." Well, yes, of course, nature (whatever that may be) has always served this purpose for the writer, and the other side of the equation—god or love or life—has always been beyond expression. "To walk abroad is, not with eyes, / But thoughts, the

*Oct 22nd 1837.*

"What are you doing now?" he asked,
"Do you keep a journal?"
"So I make my first entry to-day.

### Solitude

To be alone I find it necessary to escape
the present — I avoid myself. How could
I be alone in the Roman emperor's chamber
& mirror? I seek a garret. The spiders
must not be disturbed, nor the floor
swept, nor the timber arranged. — — —

— — The Germans say — — Es ist alles
wahr wodurch du besser wirst. — —

Thoreau's Journal, vol. 1, p. 1. "The first entry"—October 22, 1837. *Reproduced with permission of the Trustees of The Pierpont Morgan Library.*

fields to see and prize. . . ." Thoreau's fields appear in the plainest, most ordinary terms, pretty good walking and clean in the New England way. In his turn the reader moves across the gap (nature is like—) with confidence, from shrikes and chickadees, toads and snakes, wildflowers in spring and frozen apples in winter, to his most ardent aspirations. Aspirations for what? For something, not evident at first sight in the relation of shrike and chickadee. Call it perfection—"methinks a roseate sunset is preparing."

Almost more than anything else Thoreau is an inspiriting writer, and *Walden* is about the only book I know of written by a genuine author that seems to promise us happiness. "The sun is but a morning star." I say this despite the ambiguities that close analysis does turn up and the incoherence in what can only be called Thoreau's systems of thought. The devoted reader knows what Thoreau is saying, for he speaks directly to the heart, confirming what the heart already knows. Life is good. To speak otherwise is to admit personal failure. "That man who does not believe that each day contains an earlier, more sacred, and auroral hour than he has yet profaned, has despaired of life. . . ." To live well you must master the art of affecting the quality of the day. To learn this art you must know what is happening in the woods at night and at the bottom of streams and on the surface of the quaking bog. You must inspect snowstorms. You must savor the difference between the low growing and the highbush blueberry. He is telling us that life is wild, to use his favorite word, something best understood by, of all people, the red Indians, something still to be felt in the rise and fall of rivers, the flight of geese, the growth of trees, the movement and force that contains winter and death. Such knowledge brings hope and reassurance. From any other point of view this can be seen as a very strange conclusion indeed.

It really isn't very clear, and you either know what Thoreau is talking about or you don't. The art, however, is unmistakable. In the several pages at the end of *Walden* on the railroad cut in spring, a regular set piece, can be demonstrated most beautifully how complex is Thoreau's vision, how, in fact the world of thawing sand and clay becomes a symbol of life itself, for rivers, trees, butterflies, and, most wonderfully, blood vessels. The movement from the plain ordinariness of walking down the B & M tracks to seeing the earth as "living poetry" is grand enough to excite a cheer. There are also simpler examples where he does not rely on the piling up of sentence on sentence to construct a context where a larger meaning seems all but put into words. Sometimes he is simply cryptic. Three times he notices in his *Journal* without preparation or comment that corn grows in the night, and the attentive reader knows that the natural phenomenon so dear to middle western writers is really not what is being talked about. Or consider a fragment of a sentence where, it seems to me, Thoreau is at his very best: "—explore your own higher latitudes—with shiploads of preserved meats to support you, if they be necessary, and pile the empty cans sky-high for a sign." Here Thoreau uses what we take on Sunday mornings to the town dump as symbols for all we discard in our social institutions (Harvard College, the state, the family) in pursuit of our own private aspiration. But that is a stupid beginning of a translation and misses all the fun of the thing. Better leave it in the original Concord, where it is perfectly plain. Only by an effort of the historical imagination is it possible to imagine someone—like Dr. Johnson—so dull, so unwilling to understand, as to profess not to know what Thoreau is talking about. What are these higher latitudes? Why tin cans? A sign for what? Of course you could always try to explain Thoreau's meaning by talking about the search for Franklin, the search for the North-West Passage, the search for—. But no lectures on American Civilization, no close reading of the text, will ever fill in what is meant by that dash. The fact is Thoreau is conveying more than words can ever say. How, you ask, do I know this? I answer, I know that I know.

Small wonder, then, that while everyone is conscious of the limitations of language Thoreau should seem to be a very great man and a very great writer. He is telling us that life must be good, our human capacities are infinite, our inexpressible desires capable of being satisfied. He tells us all this by speaking of the ordinary things of pasture and woodlot and stream. To use his own words, he heard beyond the range of sound and saw beyond the range of sight. He lived in two worlds, and so his life was, as he said, an ecstasy.

The sad truth is that within the short lifetime of forty-five years this vision of the world and this use of language proved not to be durable. Of course Emerson in his funeral sermon tried to insure a happy ending by calling Thoreau "a spirit . . . which effaced its defeats with new triumphs." Would that this were possible, and that this language stood for some recognizable experience. As for the record of Thoreau's failure, it is all written out in the journal.

Once upon a time Thoreau gathered the wild vine of the Assabet. Finally he gathered a measurable quantity of cranberries. Once Thoreau knew that in naming and measuring—the process so satisfying to the ordinary person who gets interested in his surroundings—there is something deadly. Repeatedly he spoke of how the description of a bird or a flower killed for him the direct wordless experience of the object. Yet this vision of wild nature— "What is a man but a mass of thawing clay?"—early began to grow dim, as if it depended simply on being young, as if the failure were in the nervous system itself. Already in 1851—three years before *Walden*—he was asking himself if he were not "narrowed down to the field of the microscope." Later he asks, "Shall I become insensible as a fungus?" And he says, "We begin to die, not in our senses or extremities, but in our divine faculties." In a long passage, he places the blame partly outside himself: "We soon get through with Nature. She excites an expectation she cannot satisfy. . . . There was a time when the beauty and the music were all within, and I sat and listened to my thoughts, and there was a song in them." Along with these and similar passages there are many examples of what can only be called a hardening of the heart. His descriptions of the explosion at the powder mill, of a tree struck by lightning, of an ice storm, are beautifully exact and entirely without regard for violence as a fact, a terrifying fact. Thoreau was not, to use his own contemptuous word, a "feeling" man.

Nature had once been "all but a figure of speech," but with time, alas, the other side of the similitude grew dim and immediate experience finally became more and more fascinating for, as we say, its own sake. Ordinary names are enough for ordinary objects. So when late in life Thoreau found, of all things, three or four pieces of coral in a field near Concord, he does not immediately begin to play with the paradox of the far as near nor does he hear in the rumble of the farmer's wagon crossing a plank bridge the thunder of waves on undream'd shores. Just like anyone else he wonders how these bits of coral came there, and then he moves on to something else. Coral turns out to be coral. And what is wrong with that?

Thoreau's world finally appears as the rich multiplicity of the naturalist. This was a change of direction rather than a choice between opposites. Or to put it another way, it was a change in language, from metaphor expressing the world as a trope or symbol to a more or less technical terminology by which the parts of this world are related one to another. Channing tells us that Thoreau's dream was to compile a calendar of Concord, to "paint a sufficient panorama of the year, which multiplied the image of a day." Another noble ambition. The last volumes of the *Journal*—those printed do not contain all his observations—show him as one obsessed, moving from one thing to another in an endless succession of marvels. He recorded temperatures, the height of rivers, the depth of snow. He took muskrat houses and birds' nests apart to see how they were built and with what materials. He observed the formation of ice. And then one day while counting tree rings he caught cold.

As a story of a man's life or of a writer's career, this does not come out right, and a reader who tries to express his mixed responses to Thoreau may well feel that his dominant emotion is sadness. Here is a man who promises us everything. Consciousness alone, unaided by armies or money or dynamos or political power or tradition, can shape the world to our own expectation. The force of a single mind—if only you write an essay or hire a hall and give a lecture—can do anything. Or in simplest terms and in one of his best sentences, "To affect the quality of the day, that is the highest of arts." Why, then, should life end in counting and measuring and labeling according to Gray's *Botany?* It is hard not to feel there is some kind of defeat here.

Another way to talk about this sadness is for the reader to admit that he is thinking partly of himself and how his own literary expectations have changed. If he responds, as every good reader should do, to Thoreau's most hopeful tones, he must also recognize this susceptibility as weakness. For Thoreau's position as an author when he is talking about the new dawn is remarkable, perhaps the most remarkable thing about him. It is inexcusable. Thoreau speaks as a god.

For Thoreau is not like other men. He does not share the usual human limitations, such as an inability to understand other people, a misplaced confidence in what and how much is known to anyone, wilfulness, a pathetically invincible selfishness, a general stupidity, etc. He knows and understands and judges everything and everybody. And he speaks directly to the reader as one who shares this same godlike capability. For example, when Thoreau says, "The impression made on a wise man is that of universal innocence. Poison is not poisonous after all, nor are any wounds fatal," the reader instantly agrees, for he knows no poisons and bears no wounds, and easily shuts his eyes to what is around him. A single glance in any direction would provide plenty of contradictory evidence. Everywhere people volunteer the information that even in the nearest hills, the first rise in the ground toward the terrible mountains on the horizon, there are rattlesnakes. And history— "Julian attempted to draw the deadly weapon from his side," says Gibbon—supports the proposition that men have died of wounds. And for the fate of unfortunate humanity, living through no choice of their own in this dangerous valley, Thoreau, not a "feeling" man, wastes no compassion. Indeed for the homely and ingenious ways that other people have used to pass the time, to kill time, Thoreau feels nothing but contempt. The daily routine of dusting a collection of bric-a-brac on the mantelpiece, the laborious attempt to do good to other people, the organized pursuit of runaway slaves, the building of a railroad as far west as Fitchburg, the lifelong attempt to pay off the mortgage on the place, the shooting of muskrats and songbirds, the cutting down of every tree in sight, these and an infinite number of similar absurdities do not touch with pity a heart eagerly waiting for the new dawn. And the reader also feels disdain.

77

Thoreau appears as one who changed the object of his search. In one role he has just made an important discovery, a patch of woods really belonging to the land, going straight back to the red Indian, genuine woods, not yet cut over for firewood nor yet burned up by a couple of Harvard boys cooking a mess of fish. There, in these woods, are plenty of signs, if you will only look. There are bits of coral as well as cairns composed of empty tin cans to indicate that someone has already passed that way in pursuit of a hound, a bay horse, and a turtle dove. We have all had our losses, Thoreau was to explain, and the reader knows about that. The track leads straight away from all human habitation. But is this the way we really want to go? It would seem not. So we turn to the other Thoreau. One world at a time, he said, when he was dying.

# THE ONE AND ONLY

*GRAY BURR*

He heard the flicker drumming in the wood.
It sounded different. He began to march
In a route step nobody understood.
Oh, Emerson, perhaps, with half an eye
Cocked upward and the other fixed in starch,
Caught glimpses of him as he shambled by.

He did a lot of travelling in Concord,
Mapping his progress as he went along,
Finding a pond an ocean unexplored,
Two rivers that were never truly charted,
A stretch of beach the surveys had all wrong:
Where standard maps left off, his atlas started.

Leaving to sheep their skins, to towns their ways,
He built a school because he felt perplexed;
Enrolled, and stayed there just as many days
As needed for a general education.
First he learned, and then he wrote the text.
Next term the course was open to the nation.

Many have applied but few have finished.
And none has ever quite achieved his rank.
Originals in our day have diminished,
Are frowned on rather, knocked about, and cut.
For luck like this, Thoreau would have them thank
Whatever gods have jarred them from the rut.

# THOREAU'S PROPHETIC TESTIMONY

## PAUL LAUTER

> ... *the wise are not so much wiser than others as respecters of their own wisdom. Some, poor in spirit, record plaintively only what has happened to them; but others how they have happened to the universe, and the judgment which they have awarded to circumstances.* (A Week on the Concord and Merrimack Rivers)

FASHIONABLE THOREAU CRITICISM struggles with the analogical structure of *Walden* or sets upon Thoreau's books for Freudian symbols of Henry's quirks of mind. Critics may thus be reacting against the older views of Thoreau as the masterful preceptor of a good life down by the pond. But in reaction we have perhaps blinked the facts that however much Thoreau's works express the man, their aim is not only self-expression; nor, however artistic his pages may be, is their aim narrowly aesthetic. At risk of Walden lost do we ignore Thoreau's prophetic testimony.

No one would question, I think, that Thoreau had designs on his reader. In "Civil Disobedience" these are expressed in terms of the action to which he would provoke us:

> Action from principle, the perception and the performance of right, changes things and relations; it is essentially revolutionary, and does not consist wholly with anything which was. It not only divides States and churches, it divides families; ay, it divides the *individual,* separating the diabolical in him from the divine.

A usual approach to Thoreau would be to argue that, yes, essays like "Civil Disobedience" and "Slavery in Massachusetts" were intended to stimulate socio-political action in the reader, and therefore appeal to radical activists; that, on the other hand, *A Week* and *Walden* move by different paths toward different ends. I want here to take the view that all these works deal with the same problem, though in somewhat differing contexts, and that only by reading them together can we begin to reconcile the Thoreau of the critics with the inspiration of Gandhi and Martin Luther King.

Thoreau's central concern, stated in somewhat oversimplified terms, does not differ widely from that of other Romantic idealists —the Shelleys or Coleridges who conceived their art as a means of opening their readers to the revelations of epistemological Idealism. He wished to penetrate the "shams and delusions [that] are esteemed for soundest truths, while reality is fabulous" (*Walden,* "Where I Lived"). Having hearkened to the music of that underlying reality, he would "give a true account of it" to the world. And that account would, freeing men from their bondage to appearance and stereotype, stimulate them toward their own journey of exploration. Leaving this last step out of an account of Thoreau implicitly accuses him of a monstrous and sterile egotism; his view of the matter was that he bragged "for humanity rather than for myself." Be that as it may, I would suggest that *Walden* and "Civil Disobedience," the one operating in a primarily natural, the other in a primarily political context, can both best be understood as what I wish to call "testimonies" of Thoreau's Idealist endeavor. They both describe and enlarge upon real attempts to drive through an everyday world to a sanctuary—whether cabin or jail—where realities can be apprehended; both tell of Thoreau's return with messages of action for us. And that action does not amount just to non-violent resistance, on the one hand, and huckleberrying, on the other—these are simply partisan reductions of varying methods for achieving the single goal of the Idealist quest, the action which separates the "diabolical" in us from the "divine."

I wish to enlarge upon the approach to Thoreau I am suggesting in two ways: first, by focussing on the numerous analogies between him and the Hebrew prophets Amos, Hosea, the two Isaiahs, and Jeremiah; second, by examining some of Thoreau's stylistic devices to see how he wields them to achieve his prophetic goals. For both purposes it will be useful to understand how the word *testimony,* in its full import, can best describe the work both of the prophets and of Thoreau.

"Testimony" can mean, in a major sense, "any affirmation or declaration," a "public avowal, as of faith; profession"—as one dictionary puts it. "Testimony" can in this sense refer to affirmation either by public *action* or by a *written* or *spoken* avowal: maintaining a Peace Vigil, wearing a yoke, refusing to pay one's taxes might be "testimonies" of action; a pamphlet like A. J. Muste's *Speak Truth to Power,* Amos' critique of Israel and her neighbors (chapters I, II), "A Plea for Captain John Brown" might be literary "testimonies." Active and literary testimonies often are interdependent, so that the word can refer to a distinctive expression in public action *and* literary affirmation of one's faith. In a second major sense "testimony" can mean, particularly in the Bible (e.g., *Isaiah,* VIII, 16), the "tables of the Law," or in plural form "the precepts of God." If the senses of "testimony" as personal affirmation and as God's Law are compounded in a single usage—as in the phrase "the testimony of Isaiah"—the word will mean at once action and/or speech and that to which action and speech are referred, their "ground," to use a theological term. In effect, the meaning of "testimony" in such a usage may be understood as a kind of compound. Its nature is distinctive, more than merely the sum of its elements. Its properties are generated by the interaction of the elements of, on the one hand, action or literary record, and on the other, the Words which are Testimonies of man's "ultimate concern." I suggest that the works of the prophets and of Thoreau are "testimonies" in this complex sense.

To turn the matter another way, a prophetic *book* embodies a testimony of action and a Testimony of Law; the *Book of Isaiah* testifies to the actions of Isaiah the prophet and incorporates the Testimony, the Tables, precepts, or Torah, to which his actions are referred. Literary "testimonies" of the prophetic sort gain their power, I think, precisely by virtue of this double referent. They are overwhelming because they describe the real actions of a real man in relation to, with constant reference to, the "Testimonies" which formulate man's ultimate concern. In the case of Hebrew prophets like Isaiah or Jeremiah, were either the reality of the prophet's action or the context of *Torah* (which informs those actions with ultimate meaning) missing, the prophetic book could not have its power to engage us. Without the testimony of action it might easily fade into so many fine phrases; without the Testimony of *Torah* it might easily stumble into pointless narration of actions turning in a widening—and unhinged—gyre.

One further point about *testimony* and we are done with semantics. The word can also mean "any form of evidence, indication, etc."; this is the "testimony" of the witness in a trial. The witness is asked to present the "facts"—as he sees them—but he is also, in effect, attempting to persuade his listeners that his "testimony" is true, that they should accept his version of reality. So is it with all "testimonies." The prophet's actions are done, his words transcribed, not only in light of what *he believes* to be ultimately true, but they are also done to persuade others that they are done in light of what *is* ultimately true. The "testimony" which is a prophetic book not only embodies both the prophet's testimony of action and that which informs it, but it also attempts by its "testimony" to get its readers to accept its truths, to live by them.

The prophetic book, then, becomes an embodiment of a man's search to incarnate his ultimate values in his actions and the final means by which that man would attempt to move others toward their own testimonies to such values. I would argue that Thoreau's works are prophetic testimonies in this sense, and I wish now to pursue further the prophetic analogies.

There is often about the prophet's testimony an irritating certitude—partly a matter of his rhetorical stance, but primarily a function of the fact that, at least in his own view, he is attuned to divine harmonies. He regards himself as the *Nabi* or "mouthpiece" of a God predominantly manifest through the action of his *Ruach*, his breath, literally, or "spirit," though in idiomatic phrases like "breath of the lips" (perhaps *Isaiah* XI, 4) equivalent to the creative word of God. In the beginning it is the *ruach* moving upon the face of the deep and its Words ("Let there be....") which are instruments of creation. Again and again it is a Voice to which the prophet hearkens: a voice calling to Moses from the burning bush, a voice whispering to Samuel in the darkened Temple, the question of a voice to which Isaiah replies, the cry of a voice which the Second Isaiah answers. Revelations in most of the Hebrew Bible are remarkably auditory—even Job hears a voice from the whirlwind, although metaphorically he speaks of "seeing" the Lord, that is, reentering intimacy with Him. Surely it is a Call to which the Hebrew prophets respond, rather than a vision (man cannot see God face to face for the Hebrew)—of the sort culminating in Dante's white roseate glory. Perhaps, though we can hardly pursue the subject here, they sensed man's power to communicate as his most divine achievement (the punishment of Babel seems relevant), and in attempting to conceive divinity used this most divine category.

The prophet speaks, then, not for himself but for the Lord, who, as it is said again and again, "speaks through" him. To speak, as Jonah so painfully discovers, is one necessary testimony of the prophet: he is at once transmitting the message and imitating the method of the Lord.

So the cadences of Thoreau's voice reverberate and echo the predominantly natural music in which his books are grounded. Music, he says, "teaches us again and again to trust the remotest and finest as the divinest instinct, and makes a dream our only real experience." It is the beat of a far-off drummer which brings him to communication with the divine:

> These simple sounds related us to the stars. Ay, there was a logic in them so convincing that the combined sense of mankind could never make me doubt their conclusions. I stop my habitual thinking, as if the plow had suddenly run deeper in its furrow through the crust of the world. How can I go on, who have just stepped over such a bottomless skylight in the bog of my life? Suddenly old Time winked at me,—Ah, you know me, you rogue,—and news had come that IT was well. That ancient universe is in such capital health, I think undoubtedly it will never die. Heal yourselves, doctors; by God I live.
>
> > Then idle Time ran gadding by
> > And left me with Eternity alone;
> > I hear beyond the range of sound,
> > I see beyond the verge of sight,—
>
> I see, smell, taste, hear, feel, that everlasting Something to which we are allied, at once our maker, our abode, our destiny, our very Selves; the one historic truth, the

most remarkable fact which can become the distir
uninvited subject of our thought, the actual glory
universe; the only fact which a human being
avoid recognizing, or in some way forget or dispens

It doth expand my privacies
To all, and leave me single in the crowd.

I have seen how the foundations of the world a
and I have not the least doubt that it will stand
while. (*A Week,* "Monday")

Thoreau's play with a quotation from *Job* at the concl
passage illustrates a contrast between the Transcend
cocked in good-humored intimacy, and the Hebrew pr
ing in awed silence. Nonetheless, however differen
mode of listening—or apprehending God—it is to t       ......  ..
the "universal lyre," as he calls it in *Walden*—whether manifest
through the distant drummer, the hum of a telegraph wire, the
echo of bells, the tinkle of his hoe against a rock—that he tunes
his own speech. He can believe his life to be a "stately march to
an unheard music ... when to his fellows it may seem irregular
and inharmonious" only because he regards himself as "stepping
to a livelier measure, which only his nicer ear can detect" (to use
the phrasing from "The Service" of an image to be found in many
later works). "He will take a false step never, even in the most
arduous circumstances; for then the music will not fail to swell
into greater volume, and rule the movement it inspired."

Hearing, the prophet speaks; speaking, the prophet acts. But
his actions are more than talk. For while he recognizes the power
of language, he sees, as does Thoreau, that actions speak louder:
"The word which is best said came very near not being spoken
at all; for it is cousin to a deed which would have been better
done. It must have taken the place of a deed by some urgent necessity, even by some misfortune" ("Sir Walter Raleigh"). Actions are, then, crucial to the prophet, but that does not make him
the Man of Action; for his are not the simply "practical" activities
of the statesman or soldier or athlete, but are acts of a special
*symbolic* quality. It may be that the advice Jeremiah conveys by
taking a yoke upon his neck is practical; it may be that the prophecy contained in Isaiah's naming his son Shearjashub, "a remnant
shall return," is true; it is not, however, with practicality or verity
that we are here concerned, but with the manner in which values
and truths are rendered inescapable. It is, again, the manner of
Hosea, taking unto himself a wife of harlotry; it is the manner of
Jesus, dining with publicans and sinners; it is the manner of Thoreau, going to jail or to Walden; it is the manner of Gandhi, living
with Untouchables, wearing his homespun loincloth.

The importance of the symbolic act is less what it accomplishes
in the actual doing than its power to confront individuals with a

concrete problem which cannot easily be shunted aside as can well-meaning sentiments. Refusing his tax, Thoreau obviously cannot bankrupt the government; rather,

> my civil neighbor, the tax-gatherer, is the very man I have to deal with,—for it is, after all, with men and not with parchment that I quarrel,—and he has voluntarily chosen to be an agent of the government. How shall he ever know well what he is and does as an officer of the government, or as a man, until he is obliged to consider whether he shall treat me, his neighbor, for whom he has respect, as a neighbor and well-disposed man, or as a maniac and disturber of the peace, and see if he can get over this obstruction to his neighborliness without a ruder and more impetuous thought or speech corresponding with his action. ("Civil Disobedience")

This is, of course, partly the theory behind "Freedom Rides," but the prophet, even more than the freedom rider, has nothing practical to gain—even in the eyes of those he affronts by his testimony. His actions are manifestly "absurd," and are the more effective insofar as they are. For their very absurdity confronts the neighbor with a fact for which his ordinary categories—"What's in it for him?" "He got what he deserved!"—cannot account. And the combination of the provoking certitude of and the frequent unpleasant consequences to the perpetrator of the symbolic act prohibits an easy dismissal with "So what?" The testimony of symbolic action, grounded on the Word the prophet has received, and directed toward the norms he has encountered, raises in vivid purity the discrepancy between ordinary values and the absolutes for which the prophet claims to speak. It thus embroils the "neighbor" in a conflict which can be resolved by no easy logic, but only in the actions of his own life. He must either—and this dilemma the early Christian preachers used so well—deny the divinity of the prophet's inspiration (and this requires that he seek his own ultimate validation), or he must repent from association with the norms he had theretofore accepted.

The dramatic quality of the symbolic act, moreover, makes it ideal matter for literary development. "What was the meaning," Thoreau asks, of hoeing his beans; "why should I raise them?"

> Not that I wanted beans to eat, for I am by nature a Pythagorean, so far as beans are concerned, whether they mean porridge or voting, and exchanged them for rice; but, perchance, as some must work in fields if only for the sake of tropes and expression, to serve a parable-maker one day. (*Walden,* "The Bean-Field")

It is surely no accident that most of Thoreau's important works— e.g., *A Week,* "Civil Disobedience," *Walden*—arise from concrete experiences that he has deliberately set up, and specifically presented, as symbolic testimonies of action. These symbolic acts—launching himself on the Concord River, refusing his tax, moving to Walden—have, aside from the literary works which arise from them, inherent value as challenging testimonies. They confront us with things done, with dramatic engagements from which we can hardly escape, and for which we must then attempt some explanation, if only to satisfy our own impatience with them. But they are also of value to Thoreau because a gospel can be constructed from them, a gospel in which the reader's responses, even, or perhaps especially, his irritation, can be used to extend the reverberations of the acts, to focus their significance, to recommend their points to the reader.

This gospel of the present moment is not, one should note before passing from action to record, directed at undisciplined participation in ever-new experience. Quite the contrary, Thoreau patterns his actions far more than most other Transcendentalists: he does not overthrow, but rather establishes anew, ritual, celebration, holiday. He goes to Walden on Independence Day, meets the seasons with appropriate activity. The hoeing of beans becomes itself a ritual, the morning bath a "religious exercise." The religion of the prophets enjoined, of course, far more rituals, celebrations and holidays, which they, far from denying, sought to reinvigorate. It used to be a commonplace of Biblical criticism to set the prophets against those defenders of empty rituals and sacrifices, the priests. But it is now clear, in the work of scholars like Yehezkel Kaufmann, that the prophets protested against the emptying of ritual, not against ritual itself. For they recognized the need for these signposts pointing men beyond the factitious concerns of mundane life. "Remember the Sabbath, to keep it holy" was not rationalized as necessary to the health and welfare of the citizenry, but symbolized the participation of the divine in the regular round of human activity. The rhythms of man's life had to be founded on universal rhythms and patterns if his life were to have connection with those universals. Thoreau's rituals minister to such needs, needs which persist however differently universals may be conceived.

The nature of those universals presents one of Thoreau's greatest problems. God spoke to and revealed himself for the prophets not so much in creation as in *Torah* and in the movement of history. The Testimony of God in their books could thus be precepts and tables of the Law; and their own testimonies could reside in the acts by which they dramatized these precepts and through which they interpreted Israel's history. Moreover, to act as *Nabi* was itself to imitate the way of a God manifest primarily through his "voice." Thus in the presentation and interpretation of *Torah* the prophet testified at once to God's will and way. What he expressed and how he expressed it became mutually reinforcing: for if God did manifest himself through his Word, then a testimony in words, in precepts and commandments, could gain acceptance more readily as divine, as an imitation of God's way; and if *Torah* expressed God's will, then testimonies constantly referring to *Torah* as their source could gain acceptance as inspired by divine will. But for Thoreau, the divine way was the mysterious way of Nature, and the divine will was not revealed in any volume or finally in any collection of books or thoughts, but in the inmost self of a man deeply imbued with nature. "We know of no scripture," he writes in "A Winter Walk,"

> which records the pure benignity of the gods on a New England night. Their praises have never been sung, only their wrath deprecated. The best scripture, after all, records but a meagre faith. Its saints live reserved and austere. Let a brave, devout man spend the year in the woods of Maine or Labrador [or even Concord?], and see if the Hebrew Scriptures speak adequately to his condition and experience, from the setting in of winter to the breaking up of the ice.

It thus becomes imperative for Thoreau, if he would get his reader to believe that he was attuned to divine harmonies, to bring the reader with him to Walden to experience those natural harmonies. For his work to become a Testimony of his God, tables of divine law as he sensed it, Thoreau had to adopt Emerson's injunction: "My book should smell of pines and resound with the hum of insects." The extensive natural detail serves, in this way, an organic function in Thoreau's prophetic testimony. He can then argue that "we are enabled to apprehend at all what is sublime and noble only by the perpetual instilling and drenching of the reality that surrounds us" (*Walden,* "Where I Lived").

But mere detail could not, of course, so saturate a reader in nature itself. Thoreau marshalled all literary and rhetorical arts to serve that end. His images in particular were often drawn from and at the same time helped on the page to realize nature and locate man in it. Having surveyed in elaborate detail the geography of the ponds, he suggests a general principle: "If we knew all the laws of Nature, we should need only one fact, or the description of one actual phenomenon, to infer all the particular results at that point" (*Walden,* "The Pond in Winter"). These observations he applies to ethics, developing an elaborate metaphor that presents man himself as a pond to be plumbed and explored. The more closely we observe, the more we see ourselves organically related to nature; we learn of ourselves as we learn of nature, we discover that our laws are grounded on nature's: "The universe constantly and obediently answers to our conceptions; whether we travel fast or slow, the track is laid for us" (*Walden*, "Where I Lived"). "Shall I not have intelligence with the earth? Am I not partly leaves and vegetable mould myself?" (*Walden*, "Solitude"). Through the presentation and exploration of "correspondences" are the divine Tables in Walden hinted at; thus are we brought to sense them.

Clearly Thoreau is practicing another of Emerson's principles: ". . . picturesque language is at once a commanding certificate that he who employs it is a man in alliance with truth and God" *(Nature)*. The very use of imagery, in this view, recommends as inspired what the writer has to say to his reader, for the symbols and myths of man reverberate to the ground-tones of the universe:

> The hidden significance of these fables which is sometimes thought to have been detected, the ethics running parallel to the poetry and history, are not so remarkable as the readiness with which they may be made to express a variety of truths. As if they were the skeletons of still older and more universal truths than any whose flesh and blood they are for the time made to wear. It is like striving to make the sun, or the wind, or the sea symbols to signify exclusively the particular thoughts of our day. But what signifies it? In the mythus a superhuman intelligence uses the unconscious thoughts and dreams of men as its hieroglyphics to address men unborn. In the history of the human mind, these glowing and ruddy fables precede the noonday thoughts of men, as Aurora the sun's rays. The matutine intellect of the poet, keeping in advance of the glare of philosophy, always dwells in this auroral atmosphere. (*A Week*, "Sunday")

One of the major aims of his art and his rhetoric, as of the symbolic acts in *A Week, Walden*, "A Walk to Wachusett," is, then, to draw us into this atmosphere where his god, "that everlasting Something," can be conceived and his Tables apprehended. Further, Thoreau's elaboration of metaphors—in single sentences, whole paragraphs, indeed chapters and books—helps train his reader to think in symbolic terms, that is, in correspondential terms. If Thoreau can get his reader to envision reality in these terms, he will draw him a step further into that "auroral atmosphere"; additionally, he will shake him loose from his stereotypic responses to superficialities. Or more precisely, provoking his reader from sterile lethargy, he will engender in him, for the first time perhaps, truly significant responses to reality.

This latter purpose is Thoreau's second major aim in writing as he acted: "I do not propose to write an ode to dejection, but to brag as lustily as chanticleer in the morning . . . if only to wake my neighbors up." While one effect of his writing is to open divine nature to us, his written testimony also stimulates us to break out of the pens we have made of our lives:

> I do not wish to flatter my townsmen, nor to be flattered by them, for that will not advance either of us. We need to be provoked,—goaded like oxen, as we are, into a trot. (*Walden,* "Reading")

Not only do his works record actions which, as we saw above, designedly irritated his neighbors, but Thoreau's whole approach to recording these testimonies was more provoking still.

To drive men from their comfortable sanctimonies, Thoreau charges almost every page with exasperating remarks about Church, State, and Civilization. The tavern he compares favorably with the local church, the New Testament he sees as prejudiced against the life of Jesus because it was edited by Christians; the best government governs not at all; the railroad runs on men, who, for the most part, live mean and sneaking lives anyway. One could fill delightful pages with distillations of Thoreau's venom, but such a compilation would miss the point such remarks serve in the contexts from which we have lifted them. They are one of Thoreau's primary devices for achieving in his writing what his refusal to pay his tax achieved in his life. Rubbed by such remarks, we are continually provoked; it may be, too, that we are also jolted from uncaring shrugs toward Thoreau, that our minds, like electrical poles freed of sludge, are sensitized to the more subtle devices he uses to galvanize them. True, he takes the risk of hardening readers against him, but as preachers and psychiatrists know, chances must be taken if radical cures are to be effected. A subject must be brought to a crisis, perhaps through such challenges to his comforting norms as Thoreau's. And in any case, the kind of book Thoreau wishes to write will inevitably appear shocking:

> Books, not which afford us a cowering enjoyment, but in which each thought is of unusual daring; such as an idle man cannot read, and a timid one would not be entertained by, which even make us dangerous to existing institutions,—such I call good books. (*A Week,* "Sunday")

To make us thus "dangerous to existing institutions," Thoreau must stimulate us and educate us to penetrate to true realities beneath the veneer of conventional assumptions. It is primarily to this goal, I think, that he dedicates some of the most characteristic elements of his style: in particular, his use of paradox and word-play. While Thoreau does call upon typically Emersonian imagery of exploration (as in the "Conclusion" to *Walden*) to represent the life he would have men lead, he conceives this life less as a matter of exploring new latitudes than of seeing truly those in which we everyday sail. By using paradox and word-play Thoreau stimulates us to reconsider the true nature of words, of phrases, of the situations these describe, which we have taken for granted. Do we enjoy killing time? "As if you could kill time without injuring eternity." Are we proud of our possessions, our traps? Are they not traps altogether? How can the freer souls be in the jail, or money come between a man and his objects? Or, in a more positive and therefore rarer format, is not the growth of an ear of wheat, Latin *spica,* itself a source of hope if, as Thoreau traces it, its derivation is *speca,* from *spe,* hope? Not only through word-play, incongruity, redefinition, etymology does Thoreau lead us to review what we take to be reality; simply by contrasting related words or insisting upon a single word he may force us to reconsider their true meanings to us:

> Thus the State never intentionally confronts a man's sense, intellectual or moral, but only his body, his senses. It is not armed with superior wit or honesty, but with superior physical strength. I was not born to be forced. I will breathe after my own fashion. Let us see who is the strongest. What force has a multitude? They only can force me who obey a higher law than I. They force me to become like themselves. I do not hear of *men* being *forced* to live this way or that by masses of men. What sort of life were that to live? ("Civil Disobedience")

Just as his imagery works its magic regardless of subject, so these verbal devices operate on every page of every work to realize and convey Thoreau's testimony, and to win adherents for it.

If, then, one begins by studying the internal dynamics of all Thoreau's works, one will discover the single testimony which informs essays as apparently diverse as *Walden* and "Civil Disobedience," "Walking" and "Slavery in Massachusetts." A thorough analysis of devices like word-play, redefinition, paradox, indeed metaphor and overall structure itself, indicates that the real differences among Thoreau's works involve the impediments to Idealist exploration he wished, in any given essay, to consider how to overcome. And this analysis unifies the stylist of the critics with the inspiration of the reformers in the Idealist seer or prophet.

Such a prophet, as the epigraph to this essay suggests, happens to the universe; like Emerson's poet "he has a whole new experience to unfold," a "judgment" which he hopes will enrich and enlighten those whom he can awaken to it. As he dedicates his life in listening deep to those universal harmonies to which he alone is attuned, so he consecrates his art to transposing that music into the modes which will help attune the ears of others to their own inner harmonies. And as the value of his art is an earnest of the value of his life, so it may be that the testimony of his art cannot succeed beyond the testimony of his life. We will only learn, in Thoreau's case, as both testimonies are studied together.

# THOREAU IN ITALY

*ROBERT FRANCIS*

Lingo of birds was easier than the lingo of peasants—
they were elusive, though, the birds, for excellent reasons.
He thought of Virgil, Virgil who wasn't there to chat with.

History he never forgave for letting Latin
lapse into Italian, a renegade jabbering
musical enough but not enough to call music.

So he conversed with stones, imperial and papal.
Even the preposterous popes he could condone
a moment for the clean arrogance of their inscriptions.

He asked the Italians only to leave him in the past
alone, but this was what they emphatically never did.
Being the present, they never ceased to celebrate it.

Something was always brushing him on the street, satyr
or saint—impossible to say which the more foreign.
At home he was called touchy; here he knew he was.

Impossible to say. The dazzling nude with sex
lovingly displayed like carven fruit, the black
robe sweeping a holy and unholy dust.

Always the flesh whether to lacerate or kiss—
conspiracy of fauns and clerics smiling back
and forth at each other acquiescently through leaves.

Caught between wan monastic mountains wearing the tonsure
and the all-siren, ever-dimpling sea, he saw
(how could he fail?) at heart geography to blame.

So home to Concord where (as he might have known he would)
he found the Italy he wanted to remember.
Why had he sailed if not for the savour of returning?

An Italy distilled of all extreme, conflict,
collusion—an Italy without the Italians—
in whose green context he could con again his Virgil.

In cedar he read cypress, in the wild apple, olive.
His hills would stand up favorably to the hills of Rome.
His arrowheads could hold their own with art Etruscan.

And Walden clearly was his Mediterranean
whose infinite colors were his picture gallery.
How far his little boat transported him—how far.

# THE CONCORD ACADEMIC DEBATING SOCIETY

## DOROTHY NYREN

WALTER HARDING IN HIS *A Thoreau Handbook* says that "comparatively little is known of Thoreau's youth."[1] Most of that little is traditional family folklore. It is therefore of particular interest that recent investigation of the 1828-30 minutes of the Concord Academic Debating Society reveals several contemporary comments on Thoreau as a boy of eleven and twelve. These minutes are owned by the Concord Free Public Library and were presented to it by a Miss Carkin in 1895.

The club was established at Concord Academy while Henry Thoreau was a student there. Henry and his brother John were members along with seventeen other boys, whose age ranged from eleven to thirteen. Other boys who belonged to the club were Ebenezer Rockwood Hoar, who later became Grant's Attorney General, and William Whiting, later legal adviser to President Lincoln.

The Constitution reads as follows:

> Article 1st. This society shall be called "The Concord Academic Debating Society."
>
> Article 2nd. The disputants shall speak according to age, the oldest taking the affirmative.
>
> Article 3rd. The regular disputants shall begin by speaking twice each, then the question shall be open to the other members, who may speak twice each. The affirmative disputant may then speak and his opponent may close the question.
>
> Article 4th. There shall be no speaking except as is permitted in Article 3rd, except to correct some misstatement, or misunderstanding.
>
> Article 5th. No member shall speak while another is standing with the above exception. Every member shall seat himself as soon as he has done speaking.
>
> Article 6th. Five members shall be necessary to make a quorum.
>
> Article 7th. A Secretary shall be chosen who shall hold office three months.
>
> Article 8th. Strict order shall be enforced by the President.

---

[1] (New York: New York University Press, 1959), 2.

Article 9th. All business shall be transacted before speaking.

Article 10th. Meeting shall be called to order at 7 o'clock.

Article 11th. No member shall be dismissed without a reasonable excuse.

Article 12th. Every member shall either speak himself, or procure one to speak for him.

To this admirable constitution are added fifteen by-laws, the most interesting of which is that every member absenting himself without a reasonable excuse shall light up the room (i.e. pay for the lamp oil) for the two following evenings.

At the first meeting on October 7, 1828, William Whiting was elected Secretary. His notes for the next seven meetings are kept in admirable form but include no mention of Henry Thoreau beyond the fact of his membership. In December the club made choice of Josiah G. Davis as Secretary and "forced him to accept." Master Davis' notes leave much to be desired in the way of spelling and legibility. Again Henry Thoreau's name is conspicuous by its absence.

In September of the following year George Moore became Secretary. Henry Thoreau was then twelve years old and was called upon to participate more actively in the proceedings. As the minutes show, his response was minimal enough to be termed negative.

The first entry which speaks of Thoreau arguing in a debate reads as follows:

Friday Oct. 9, 1829

The club was called to order at about ½ past 6 o'clock. There were a few declamations. The record was then read. "Does it require more talents to make a good writer than a good extemporaneous speaker?" was discussed by H. Thoreau Aff. and E. R. Hoar Neg. The debate was not very animated this evening, on account of some misunderstanding in the question. The President decided in the Negative, and upon an appeal his decision was confirmed by a majority of four. . . .

Henry Thoreau did not distinguish himself at that meeting; he did much worse on November 5. As George Moore reports it:

The discussion of the question selected for debate next followed, "Is a good memory preferable to a good understanding in order to be a distinguished scholar at school?" E. Wright Aff. H. Thoreau Neg. The affirmative disputant, through negligence, had prepared nothing for debate, and the negative, not much more. Accordingly, no other member speaking, the President decided in the Neg. His decision was confirmed by a majority of four. Such a debate, if it may be called so, as we have had this evening, I hope never again will be witnessed in this house, or recorded in this book. It is not only a waste of time, but of paper to record such proceedings of wood and oil.

The preceding comment is of particular interest because the secretaries had in general limited themselves to recording proceedings and had seldom made statements of this sort before.

The final comment on Thoreau is recorded by George Moore on December 17, 1829.

The Secretary being absent, Henry Thoreau was chosen Sec. pro. tem. and he neglecting to perform his duty by recording the proceedings, it falls to the lot of the Sec. to record by hearsay what was done.

It will be noted that only one secretary, George Moore, mentioned Thoreau. George Moore seems to have been one of the more serious and responsible members of the club. In October, 1829 he was chosen to be treasurer and to purchase lamps for the group. Among the Concord Academy compositions which Hubert H. Hoeltje cites in "Thoreau and the Concord Academy"[2] is a composition by George Moore supporting the proposition that, "Whatever is, is right." Quite possibly Thoreau and Moore were of such opposite temperaments that Moore could not help being prejudiced against him. Nevertheless, these statements by a contemporary, worded in a forthright boyish way, cannot be ignored.

Besides the light these entries shed on Thoreau's character and inclinations, several other bits of minor information are contributed by the minutes. Thoreau is regularly referred to as Henry or H. Thoreau by the boys of the club, although he was still habitually referred to as David in the official records of the school. We therefore see him on the very verge of changing his name.

Further data as to when he actually began attending Concord Academy is also given. Mr. Hoeltje says, "Henry Thoreau himself, as nearly as one can judge . . . first enrolled in the Concord Academy for the quarter ending on February 25, 1829."[3] Since Thoreau is listed as a member before the first entry for October 7, 1828, it can be safely said that Thoreau was at the Academy on that date.

The type of question debated by the group is of some interest as revealing matters of intellectual concern to those with whom Thoreau associated in his formative years. In addition to the topics

---

[2] *The New England Quarterly*, XXI (March, 1948), 103.
[3] *Ibid.*, 104.

already referred to, the club also discussed "Do children imbibe and imitate virtue as readily as vice?" This and other questions all were to be much discussed by Thoreau, Emerson, and Bronson Alcott in the years to come. We had not known before that they had all been presented for Thoreau's consideration while he was still a school boy.

The last bit of information that can be gleaned from the minutes is that the Debating Society may be a precursor of the Lyceum and, if not that, one can at least say that its course began before the Lyceum and ceased shortly after the Lyceum was founded. George Moore refers to a "new club" in his last entry in the minutes and we find that four and possibly five of the eleven members of the Debating Society who were Concord residents are listed as original members of the Lyceum.[4] Neither of the Thoreau brothers are included in this list so we may assume that neither Henry nor John had found the Debating Society's meetings rewarding enough to convince them that participation in the town's Lyceum would suit their talents and interests.

---

[4] *Proceedings of the Fiftieth Anniversary of the Organization of the Concord Lyceum* (Concord, Mass., 1879), 30.

# THE THOREAU ROMANCE

## LOUISE OSGOOD KOOPMAN

DURING MY YOUTH I always traveled with a huge trunk, such as were used in the last century, inscribed at each end in large letters, S. D. Thoreau. As the Thoreau family in America had died out, I felt rather like the last of the Romans or of the Mohicans.

And I was not a Thoreau. The trunk had fallen to my use years after the death of Sophia Thoreau, who had left to my mother a small legacy and all her personal possessions.

These personal possessions came in this trunk.

The friendship between the Thoreaus and the Wards was of long standing.

My great-grandmother, Prudence Ward, was a widow for many years and spent the last years of her life as a boarder or paying guest with the Thoreaus in Concord.

At first her two daughters were with her, but Caroline—my grandmother—soon met and married Edmund Quincy Sewall, who was studying divinity with Dr. Ripley at the Old Manse in Concord. I like to think that my grandfather Sewall occupied the funny little attic chamber called the "Parson's Room."

Edmund Sewall became one of our early Unitarian ministers. He was considered to be a brilliant, scholarly man, but was always in poor health. Before very long the Sewalls became the parents of Ellen Devereux Sewall, my mother. Devereux was a family name, but Ellen came from the heroine of Walter Scott's poem. My grandparents were young and romantic.

After several years my grandfather was installed as the Unitarian minister in Scituate, where my mother grew up.

Prudence Ward, the elder sister, remained at the Thoreau's until the death of her mother. My great-grandmother Ward now lies in the Sleepy Hollow Graveyard in Concord.

Concord at that time must have been a pleasant place for the Wards to settle down in. It was the period of what may be called the Golden Age of Concord.

New ideas were in the air and old dogmas were being questioned.

Emerson was writing his philosophy. Lyceum Lectures were eagerly welcomed far and wide. Alcott had the courage of his ideas, Hawthorne brooded and wrote, and Henry Thoreau walked and thought.

The young people did not fare badly.

Of course there was no dancing nor card playing, but youths

and maidens met at supper parties, picnics, Sunday singings around the piano or organ.

There were meetings and lectures galore, after which arose the serious question as to which youth would take which girl home. And from reading the correspondence between Maria Thoreau, Henry Thoreau's aunt, and my grandmother, Caroline Ward, both young girls at the time, I should judge that this generation was just as silly and no sillier than one's own, whichever generation one happens to belong to.

This was the romantic age. All young girls kept diaries, copied poems, pressed flowers, painted, and above all, wrote each other long, long letters—no telephones at that time!

The Thoreau family does not appear to have been intellectual. Certainly "Aunt Maria," as my mother was taught to call her, was not, although she had sterling qualities.

The Wards evidently were. Prudence Ward, whom I remember, read much, always took the *Dial,* gardened, botanized and painted really lovely flowers.

And the Wards soon had connections in Concord. Alcott's wife was a cousin of Edmund Sewall ("poor Cousin Abby" as she was always termed in the family) and Emerson's first wife was some sort of cousin of his.

Naturally my grandmother Sewall often visited her mother and sister, and later she would bring her daughter Ellen. And Ellen grew to be a childhood friend of the two Thoreau girls, Sophia and Helen. Later Ellen could make these visits by herself. They apparently lasted for a month.

Concord and Scituate were far apart in those days. First the stagecoach to Boston, a night spent with relatives there and another coach trip to Concord were necessary.

It seems to have been a friendly way of traveling. The passengers all told their names, usually the reason for their trip, and often had common connections or friends. One thinks of Dickens's descriptions of coach travel in England.

The one visit that is of especial interest was made when Ellen was seventeen years old.

I must mention here that my mother, according to all accounts, was a beautiful girl. As she was over forty when I was born the youngest of ten children—I am now 98 years old—I can speak only of her sympathy and imagination, and of course, to me she was beautiful. I know that we five sisters, a good looking lot, were always told that we were not as pretty as our mother. We loved it.

At the wedding of a sister when my mother was in the sixties, a guest remarked that Mrs. Osgood (my mother) was the handsomest woman in the church. I treasured that remark for I had induced my mother to wear a lovely cap and she hated caps. Ladies could be regal in those days in their heavy black silks and trains.

So it is hardly to be wondered at that the two Thoreau young men, John and Henry, felt her charm. The Thoreau sisters, Sophia and Helen (who died not long afterward), were away at school. It must have been June.

But the two young men were at home. They naturally devoted themselves to the entertainment of the pretty young girl.

Many walks were taken, rows on the Concord River, hills climbed for views, woods explored. There is a legend that they carved their initials on a tree. There was endless talking too, evidently mostly by Henry with the others asking him questions. These expeditions were always accompanied by Ellen's Aunt Prudence who must have been young at the time and I fancy enjoyed her duty as chaperone.

It seems to have been always sunny and warm.

The little love affair which followed would be of no interest outside the family except that one of the young men became a distinguished writer.

The Thoreau sisters returned after two weeks and that visit came to an end.

But the friendship between the young people did not. Little visits to Scituate were made by John and Henry.

John seems to have made a pet of Ellen's little brother George, then about five years old, while it must have been at this time that Henry wrote his poem "To a Gentle Boy," after meeting Ellen's 11 year old brother Edmund Sewall. That poem is sometimes mistakenly recorded as written to, or of, Ellen herself. My uncle Edmund was always ashamed of the poem, but his descendants value the manuscript of it highly.

One would know more of this period if my dear mother had not cut out from her diary all mention of the Thoreau brothers. It is pleasant to me to know that my mother had such delicate feelings, but one can't help wishing that she had kept those items in.

It was the following summer when John made his last visit to Scituate.

Ellen and John walked along beautiful Scituate beach. Miss Ward was with them, of course, but she obligingly rested on a rock while the young pair walked.

John asked Ellen to marry him. She accepted him, but when she returned home she felt doubtful and uncertain as to whether it was not Henry whom she cared for.

She was very young, and she felt almost in love with both.

So when her father, to whom John had gone, objected to the

match she was glad to change her answer. I have never understood my grandfather's attitude. Perhaps his refusal came from the fact that both John and Henry were rumored to be transcendentalists. He has always been depicted to me as a saint and yet the stupidest saint might realize that young people do fall in love. And yet he sent his elder son to the school which the two Thoreaus soon afterwards started.

My grandfather appears to have been busy during my mother's early youth in shooing away aspirants to her hand. My mother once told me that when my father offered himself she accepted him on the spot.

Soon after John's offer, while Ellen was feeling miserably ashamed of herself, she was sent to visit her uncle Henry Sewall in Watertown, New York, where a branch of the Sewall family lived. Mary Sewall, a daughter of Henry, had been with her at boarding school during their early teens.

I have always fancied that this visit was planned by her parents as a means of getting her away from the Thoreau young men.

However, soon after Ellen arrived at Watertown she received a letter from Henry Thoreau. He asked her to marry him.

I have heard that it was a "remarkable and beautiful" letter, but it was destroyed either by Ellen or her father. The poor girl was still ashamed and "mixed up" in her feelings, but she wrote and refused Henry. A letter which she wrote at this time to her aunt has been kept. In it she expressed regret that her father had not been with her to help her write to Henry, but that she had answered his letter as well as she could.

This was the end of the love affair. John died at 28. Ellen writes of her sorrow over the past so soon ended, and that she could not write more. Her friendship with Sophia Thoreau was kept up, as well as her mother's friendship with Aunt Maria who wrote frequent and voluminous letters.

I can just remember Sophia visiting us. My sister Fanny remembers that she told us to call her Aunt Sophia but my only remembrance of her is that she had a bad headache and that green tea was sent out for her as she could not drink our black tea. One's memory is a curious thing!

A year later my mother's mistakes over her Thoreau love affair did not prevent her from noticing the now Unitarian minister, Joseph Osgood, fresh from the Harvard Divinity School, who had just been ordained in the old church in Cohasset. Cohasset and Scituate were neighboring towns.

Naturally the two young people saw much of each other and this time when my father offered himself Ellen had no doubt.

They were married when Ellen was twenty-two and, as the

story books say, lived happily ever after—truer in this case than in many. It was a lively, happy household and a busy one.

My mother dearly loved my father. I think that later on in her quiet moments the Thoreau love affair occupied a separate niche in her mind dear to remember.

My sister Fanny (Frances) and I came after a pause in babies, and my mother had more time to tell us stories. She told them delightfully.

Her father had started teaching her Greek when she was six years old but had left off the teaching of Greek to replace it with logic when she was eleven. It seems a queer plan.

As we grew older she told us much about the Thoreau family.

Mr. Thoreau was a friendly, quiet man, not saying much and busy with his own affairs. One can hardly wonder at that, for Mrs. Thoreau (a Dunbar and a thorough Yankee) was an inveterate talker, and then there was Aunt Maria, not to mention the Wards.

She told us little that I remember about the young people. But I do recall one incident; when they were both children Sophia visited her at her grandmother Sewall's in Boston. The little girls grew tired of playing by the Frog Pond and Ellen, the hostess, offered to show Sophia the State House. She did so, inside and out. Unobserved, the two little girls climbed up among the beams inside the dome until they reached the top. It was a dangerous thing to do. Many years later Sophia asked my mother whether it was a dream or true.

We children had always heard vaguely of the "Thoreau Love Affair" as we called it, although not from my mother.

At an early age it was my task to dust our sitting room. In one corner of it stood a "what-not," on one shelf of which was a row of books. Among them was a set of Thoreau's works, given to my mother by my oldest sister and brother who were then out in the world. As I was an eager reader I dipped into all these books, and as I found the Thoreau books dull with no pictures, I lost all interest in them or in him.

Instead, I was much more interested in his brother John who had died at 28. John's death was caused by his stepping on a rusty nail, getting lockjaw and dying, a story told to us for the purpose of making us more careful where we stepped.

I think I wished that it had been Henry instead of John. I imagined John as a beautiful youth, perhaps because he died so young.

Later the arrival of Sophia Thoreau's trunk interested us. As I remember, it contained mostly letters, books, papers, notebooks, and such things. There was an oval frame containing a photograph of Bronson Alcott, which, as Alcott's wife's family did not care much for him, was hung behind a door in the parlor.

And there was a brilliant Roman Striped shawl. It was hard to imagine quiet Sophia wearing that to Sunday meeting. But the main value of the collection was in the writings and letters. Unluckily my youngest brother at that time collected stamps and some of the later letters must have been lost.

Long afterward, when I was in my twenties and the Thoreau love affair dim in my memory, my mother felt moved to tell me the whole story. It was a gray misty Sunday afternoon. We were alone in the house, except for my father who was in his study upstairs reading or perhaps taking a nap after preaching his Sunday sermon.

I was writing letters and my mother came in. Something must have recalled the Thoreaus to us, and I think my mother was glad to tell me the story. We were very close. I wish that I could remember it better, but it made a great impression on me.

First she spoke of that wonderful visit and confessed ruefully that she felt sorry when the Thoreau girls returned. She told of their many walks and talks. And of that walk with John, of his offer and of the shame that she felt afterwards. I am ashamed to say that I cannot remember what she said about Henry's offer, but I know that we spoke much of it. A walk on a beach, with an offer, at that time, was more romantic to me than a letter.

It was not a long talk, and during much of it I was asking my mother questions.

I asked her if Henry knew that John had asked her to marry him. She replied that Sophia told her that after John died she had mentioned to Henry John's wanting to marry Ellen. Henry remarked, "Did John love her too?"

I also asked if she knew whether Henry continued to care for her. Sophia had told her that shortly before Henry's death, probably in answer to some remark of hers, Henry had said, "I have always loved her".

As I have grown older, I have concluded that Henry may have cherished the love or perhaps the memory of it. It showed him to himself as a human being as well as a philosopher.

And also in thinking over what my mother had told me I feel that it was Henry whom she at this time loved. But of course John's tragic death moved her deeply.

My mother in that talk mentioned that Sophia was always annoyed that the public seemed to think that Emerson supported Thoreau. What with his writings, lectures and the small pencil industry in which he helped his father, Henry was able to leave his sister in comfortable circumstances. I remember my mother bringing home a number of these pencils.

I am afraid that I can remember no more of this talk, but earlier my mother had told us many tales of the Thoreaus.

Phrenology was the rage and "bumps" on one's head meant much. One evening the young group amused itself testing heads. Henry, feeling for bumps on my mother's head, announced that she had none. She had a beautifully shaped head. There was much gaiety, for according to phrenology she was either a genius or an idiot.

She spoke once of reproaching Henry for not going with them to church. His reply was, "All outdoors is a church," or perhaps "All outdoors should be a church." I have forgotten which.

Aunt Maria's letters to my grandmother tell much about the Thoreaus. She was a valiant woman and evidently Henry tried her patience. She writes in one letter, "Henry is always taking walks." And in another she writes, "Henry has written a book. He has named it Walden. The name is the best part of the book." I wish I had known Aunt Maria, although she did embarrass her nieces by trying to beat down prices when they went shopping with her.

Our last connection with the Thoreau family came when I was about sixteen or seventeen.

My mother received a letter and a small package from Maria Thoreau, who was spending her last years in Portland, Maine with Dunbar cousins. She wrote that as she was the last of the Thoreaus she was sending to my mother little presents and keepsakes that she had received from my grandmother. The package contained bookmarks and trifles that I have forgotten. Maria Thoreau died not long afterwards, and thus ended the Thoreau family in America.

A few days after my mother's sudden death at seventy, for the first and only time my father referred to my mother's early love affair.

We were alone together and feeling very sad. He spoke of it and queried thoughtfully and wistfully whether my mother had had a happier life with him. I assured him that she had—and I meant it.

# THE HALF-HIDDEN THOREAU

## CARL BODE

AS I SEE IT there are three lives of Henry David Thoreau. The first is the conventional one. It inhabits the encyclopedias, the polite biographies, and the world of American literary folklore. The second is marked by some dispute and doubt; its two great areas of argument concern Thoreau's relationship with Emerson's wife and the timing of Thoreau's growth and decline as a literary artist. The third is so controversial that it has only been hinted at in print; it is Thoreau's unconscious life. Now, a century after his death, he is one of the world figures in American literature and it would seem that whatever furthers our understanding of him and his work ought to be brought out.

Emerson, the man who knew Thoreau best, once spoke of his "simple and hidden life." Simple it was, in the sense of being Spartan, and hidden too in ways no biographer has published. This is not to say that there was scandal in Thoreau's life; it is that his subconscious side has largely gone unstudied. The insights and valuable hypotheses of Freudian psychology have been ignored in the various biographies. Time has modified some of Sigmund Freud's constructions; fresh research has upset some of his analogies. But there is little doubt that we can comprehend Thoreau better if we take his unconscious into account. The finicky critic is put off, even today, by the Freudian emphasis on sexuality. The Freudian stress on childhood experience may seem unwarranted. And the very fact that there is a Freudian jargon can prejudice the reader. Yet the life of Thoreau remains full of riddles and the writing of Thoreau abounds in nuances that still need to be understood. The only Freudian study of any length is an unpublished doctoral dissertation done five years ago by Raymond Gozzi.[1] Most of its deductions come from an analysis of the imagery in Thoreau's writing, the rest from an interpretation of certain biographical data. By following Gozzi's remarkable findings we can put Thoreau into another perspective, look at him from one more point of view. It is not at all impossible that we will see things we may not wish to see. For our conclusion will be that Thoreau was not a normal man—though his writing was the richer for it.

To the Freudian, abnormality is mainly a matter of degree. Other children suffer the shocks that Thoreau doubtless did; other

---

[1] *Tropes and Figures: A Psychological Study of David Henry Thoreau.* New York University, 1957. Publication #21,762. Microfilm #57-2490, University Microfilm, Ann Arbor, Michigan.

John Thoreau, Sr. (1787-1859), Henry's father · *courtesy of Concord Free Public Library · photo by Alfred W. Hosmer, Concord*

Ellen Sewall, in her middle twenties · detail from a daguerreotype
*reproduced by permission of her daughter, Mrs. Francis W. Collier*

John Thoreau, Jr. (1814-1842), Henry's brother · from an oil portrait
by Henry's sister, Sophia · *courtesy of Concord Antiquarian Society*

Helen Thoreau (1812-1849), Henry's sister · *courtesy of Concord
Free Public Library · photo by Alfred W. Hosmer, Concord*

Diploma awarded to Thoreau and his father in 1847 at the fair of The
Massachusetts Charitable Mechanics Association · *courtesy of*

youths and men endure the same frustrations. Yet few others react as vehemently. It is normal for a boy to replay the Oedipus myth, to wish to marry his mother and obliterate his father, and then to be maimed by his unconscious feeling of guilt. It is not normal to have the effects linger throughout manhood and maturity. Much can be explained in Thoreau by assuming that they did, however.

A highly aware observer of his own psyche, he sensed what had happened to him and projected it on others. "How many men," he once exclaimed, "meet with some blast in the moist growing days of their youth, and what should have been a sweet and palatable fruit in them becomes a mere puff and excrescence!" He realized that he had been warped. Under the rubric of "Chastity and Sensuality" he collected many of his thoughts and enclosed them in a letter to his disciple H. G. O. Blake. "I send you the thoughts," Thoreau wrote, "with diffidence and shame, not knowing how far . . . I betray my peculiar defects." The salient defect, to the Freudian, was that Thoreau never outgrew his mother-fixation. It was ambivalent, with some hate supporting the love, in the typical way of the unconscious. Cynthia Thoreau dominated her husband and children, outliving them all, incidentally, except for one daughter. When Henry before leaving college asked her what profession he should choose, she answered him pleasantly, "You can buckle on your knapsack, and roam abroad to seek your fortune"; and tears came to his eyes. With the imputed exception of a girl named Ellen Sewall, young women failed to interest him even when he was a young man. He could see the reason for looking at pretty girls but not for trying to talk with them. He was not always cold to them, of course. However, from their point of view, the matter was summed up when Elizabeth Hoar remarked that, as for taking Henry's arm she would as soon think of taking the arm of an elm tree.

With an older woman Thoreau could be more responsive. There was above all Lidian, Ralph Waldo Emerson's severely beautiful wife; and she was nearly fifteen years his senior. He once wrote to her, "You must know that you represent to me woman." She remained, if by default, the principal love of his life. Yet it is worth remembering that another older woman preceded her. She was Lidian's own sister. To Mrs. Lucy Jackson Brown, three years older than Lidian, he sent his best youthful effort, the poem "Sic Vita," along with a bunch of violets. Mrs. Brown joined the Thoreau family at intervals over a period of several years. She and Henry found no dearth of things to say when they met, and when distance separated them they corresponded. The correspondence included a good deal of platonizing though not quite enough for Henry's taste. "Dear Friend," he suggested in one letter, "We always seem to be living just on the brink of a pure and lofty intercourse." He meant not only himself and Lucy Brown but the world. With Lidian the brink was passed more than once. Thoreau continued to be attracted to older women rather than younger ones; and up to the end he kept his devotion to his mother.

Because nothing in his culture could countenance a mother-fixation, Thoreau sought to shift its psychic energies to other ends. One was the attachment to older women. The other, with bountiful creative results, was his writing. There he adapted and extended the idea of Mother Nature until it became one of his chief conceptions. Kind, lovely, she let him immerse his loneliness and tension in her. Yet in her kindness and love she could be strict as a mother is strict. "In her most genial moment her laws are . . . steadfastly and relentlessly fulfilled." In Freudian terms this is Nature as the superego, the conscience. This is Cynthia Thoreau demanding obedience. Out of a loving, strict Nature Henry's needs were met, or so he maintained. The attitude he took is exemplified in a telling image: "I make it my business to extract from Nature whatever nutriment she can furnish me. . . . I milk the sky and the earth."

*Alma Natura* appeared both in his ideas and their expression. The amount of female matter in his nature writing is remarkable. Perhaps the most illuminating thing is his love for swamps. He enjoys being in them, enjoys writing about them. His friend Ellery Channing, who walked with him as often as anyone, noted the interest in swamps and bogs. It proved to be long-lived. As early as 1840 Thoreau could rhapsodize, "Would it not be a luxury to stand up to one's chin in some retired swamp for a whole summer's day?" And as late as 1857 he could still write with relish, "Methinks every swamp tends to have or suggests . . . an interior tender spot. The sphagnous crust that surrounds the pool is pliant and quaking, like the skin or muscles of the abdomen." Sometimes the subject or the imagery was masculine. The male too could find analogue and metaphor in Thoreau's writing. Throughout the pages on nature there are many references, masculine and feminine, overt and covert, which have a Freudian significance. The towering pine, the shrub oak, the snake in the stream, the unclimbable mountain: these are among them. At its apex Thoreau's sexual energy emerges as a desire for mystic union with nature. This is clearest perhaps in his poem "The Thaw":

> Fain would I stretch me by the highway-side,
> To thaw and trickle with the melting snow,
> That mingled soul and body with the tide,
> I too may through the pores of nature flow.

Beyond the domain of nature and nature's sexual images, Thoreau's energy was channeled into ideas about friendship and into their figurative expression. The ideas at the conscious level were austere, for Thoreau set a superhumanly high standard at the conscious level. At the unconscious level it can be guessed that they were marked by an incipient homosexuality. The same mother-fixation that barred a normal sexual partnership with a woman also prejudiced a normal friendship with a man by charging it with undue emphasis and tension. Such a friendship Thoreau never had. We can recall the judgment Emerson pronounced: "No equal companion stood in affectionate relations with one so pure and guileless."

To make up for his deficiency Thoreau consistently showed far more than the usual amount of aggressiveness and independence. It is indeed in a combination of the two that the world has come to recognize the stance typical of him. The literary results have been brilliant, *Walden* and "Civil Disobedience" most notably; but there are four or five other essays, such as "Life without Principle" and "Slavery in Massachusetts," which radiate those qualities. The act of writing as well as what was written stem from his aggressiveness and independence. He had to prove himself. He made a point of doing so by word and deed.

The roots of this attitude can be traced back to his earliest years. We may remember that he was a grave, withdrawn child. As a boy he was called "The Judge." Some friends of his family thought he resembled an Indian in his iron demeanor. Before college he belonged to a debating society where he often showed himself cross-grained. In his college days he was known to unbend at times but he customarily kept to himself. And so he did during the rest of his life. One reason for the attitude lies, in all probability, in the Oedipal conflict; his reserved demeanor, I believe, resulted mostly from the strength of his repressions. From the outset his unconscious urge to displace his father and enjoy his mother must have been unusually keen. And yet his developing superego, his implanted conscience, certainly asserted that this was sinful. Here we see the typical Freudian ambivalence, which would flourish in Thoreau. Here is hate for the father, but also love for him and shame for wanting to displace him. Here is the ancestor of the more general love-hate which became a staple of Thoreau's life and works. The two emotions are aspects of one, as Thoreau himself testified.

Because of inadequacies in his father and himself which we can guess at, he felt compelled to search for a father-substitute. His father, John Thoreau, Sr., was a mechanic and a bumbling businessman. He relished the crowded company of his fellows. No introverted scholar, he was still not quite strong enough to make Henry want to identify with him through fear. The search for the father took several forms during Thoreau's life but was always tinged—except at the end when John Brown satisfied Thoreau's deepest requirements—with hostility and even hate. No satisfactory God as Father could be found in Thoreau's religion. No satisfactory father could be found among his relatives or teachers. There was not even one among Thoreau's older friends and this in spite of the fact that the number included Emerson. But Emerson clearly came the closest.

When Thoreau at twenty returned to Concord to live, Emerson was thirty-four. The enormous influence he had on Thoreau was not only mental but physical. Understandably, the first impact was the greatest. James Russell Lowell, for instance, a classmate of Thoreau's at Harvard, wrote dryly in 1838: "I met Thoreau last night, and it is exquisitely amusing to see how he imitates Emerson's tone and manner. With my eyes shut, I shouldn't know them apart." Yet when he was nearly forty Thoreau could still wear his collar turned over like Emerson's. Although Emerson's influence would diminish and Thoreau would certainly become his own man, it is easy to see why he was originally impressed. Emerson was by all accounts an American saint. Bronson Alcott, most captious of the Transcendentalists, testified that his friendship with Emerson was "the greatest prize and privilege" he enjoyed aside from his family life. That was praise from somebody who knew him intimately, but even his lecture audiences recognized that they were listening to a most impressive man. In view of the widespread admiration Emerson commanded, it is the more revealing to see Thoreau gradually reject him. The love for him as father in Thoreau's heart is more and more offset by hate. Or if hate is too strong a word, then by a growing and carping hostility; or, to put it at its mildest as Thoreau tried to, by a "certain bitter-sweet sentiment." However, I think we could stand by the word "hate," for with the passing of time Thoreau added the classic Freudian incentive to hate when he fell in love with Lidian, with the wife of his father-substitute. The Oedipal drama played itself out in full, leaving him to fight a painful sense of shame.

So far in our examination of Thoreau's unconscious we have been saying that its main characteristic was a marked Oedipus complex which aborted his emotional life but richly informed his writing. It made him look for a mother in older women instead of a mate and look for a father in Emerson (and later John Brown). It allowed him to compensate, however, by developing an extraordinary aggressiveness and independence; and it allowed him to sublimate through literary creation.

Now we have three more propositions to advance. One is that Thoreau's hatred for the state was an extension of his Oedipal hatred for his father and of his occasional dislike (the other side of the coin of love) of his dominating mother. Another is that he finally found his father-substitute in John Brown, as the fanatical leader who detested the state and defied it to the death. The last is that Thoreau, with a history of conversion maladies, found his burden of guilt so great when his father and Brown died, both within the same year, that he became convinced he too must die in expiation. Each of these three can be supported from Freudian psychology, although certain evidence is lacking and the likelihood of the propositions must be based partly on the previous constructions.

We can safely conclude that Thoreau resented parental authority. To understand his resentment of his father we need to look again at the character of John Thoreau, Sr. There is ground for stressing that he was not merely the mild man married to Cynthia Thoreau. Professor Gozzi suggests in his dissertation that the older Thoreau was capable of violent speech if not violent action, that he had an air of some firmness and determination, and that he was well respected outside his house. Though he was more of a man outside his house than inside, even there he proved strong enough to get his son to play Apollo to his own King Admetus. He managed, that is, to involve the reluctant Henry in the family business from time to time and when his father died Henry was forced to succeed him in charge of it. Accordingly, he had qualities that could increase his son's unconscious resentment. He stood, in essence, for the talky, noisy world of trade which Thoreau despised. Much as Thoreau loved his mother he could also be irked by her authority on occasion. More than one passage in his *Journal* suggests his animosity. And he had hard things as well as kind ones to say about parents in general. It is probable that he suppressed many of the criticisms of his father and mother. Yet there are at least a few times when he could not restrain his bitterness. Surely he was looking at his own household as well as others when he cried, "The fathers and the mothers of the town . . . don't want to have any prophets born into their families—damn them!"

For Thoreau it was only a step from resentment of the authority of the parent to resentment of the authority of the state. The first recorded conflict came when the state, according to Thoreau, "commanded me to pay a certain sum toward the support of a clergyman." He declined, although another man saw fit to pay it for him. He had made his point, however, and was never dunned for the church tax again. At the request of the state's nearest representatives, the selectmen of Concord, Thoreau prepared a declaration for their files: "Know all men by these presents, that I, Henry Thoreau, do not wish to be regarded as a member of any incorporated society which I have not joined." This sweeping affirmation represented another victory but not a permanent one. For Thoreau after declining for six years to pay a second tax, his poll tax, was put in jail on that account. A little of the edge was taken off that battle too, it must be admitted, because someone else, once again, paid the tax. But not before Thoreau had the opportunity to pass his memorable night in jail. When he wrote about it later he tinged his words with amusement and contempt for authority. However, his jailer reported that Thoreau was "mad as the devil" when released. Fighting audaciously against the state, he had been punished like a stubborn child, by being shut up. His imprisonment helped to embitter and harden Thoreau to such an extent that in the next decade he could approve of armed rebellion, of war itself. And that was what John Brown determined to wage against the United States of America.

He waged it on rocklike principle, to Thoreau's absolute satisfaction. He had already met Brown, we know, and been impressed by him two years before the attack on Harper's Ferry. But the chain of events beginning with the assault and ending with Brown's being hanged on December 2, 1859 stirred Thoreau almost incredibly. Ellery Channing reported that Thoreau's "hands involuntarily clenched together at the mention of Captain Brown." There can be little doubt that the strongest aggressions in him found an outlet through Brown. He identified himself with Brown and fought by empathy at his side. So strong did the empathy prove that, after briefly considering that Brown was dead before his trial, Thoreau refused to accept the idea that Brown was dead at all. He was not speaking metaphorically when he said, "I heard, to be sure, that he was hung, but I did not know what that meant." When he wrote and spoke passionately for Brown he was also justifying himself. And justification was needed, it may be assumed, for Thoreau could realize that Brown's hanging was the greatest punishment the state could inflict. In his stormy ambivalence Thoreau no doubt felt that Brown was completely right but also that the punishment he suffered was a judgment. It was a mistaken one to Thoreau but a judgment nonetheless. In one sense as Brown had failed so had he. In a feverish resolution of the problem he likened Brown to a Christ crucified by the state for the slaveholder.

We come now to the last and most controversial of the three propositions: that Thoreau died because he felt he should—and died content. I agree with the past biographers that on the conscious level he died of tuberculosis; and so I have said elsewhere. But I agree with Professor Gozzi that at the unconscious level Thoreau ended his life of his own accord. He was convinced that he had to die chiefly because John Brown and his father had died. He had to expiate his intolerably increasing load of guilt. Christian contrition was not for him but leaving life represented ample expiation.

If this seems unbelievable to admirers of Thoreau, we can look back into his life to find out if anything there has a bearing on the matter. By first noting that his family had a history of lingering illness—typically the Thoreaus were said to die from consumption —we can isolate a physical factor which would make it easier for the psychic ones to operate. On the psychic side we can start, ordinarily enough, with the child who became sick at thunder storms. About Thoreau's health during his boyhood we cannot be sure but we know that he was sick in college. When he was nineteen he wrote to a Harvard classmate that his health was so much improved that he would return next term; the letter was written in August 1836. In February 1841 he had another siege of illness, probably having to do with his lungs. During the next year he experienced a case of illness through empathy which is a classic. For when his brother John died in January 1842 after bitter suffering, Henry suffered too. Shortly after John's death Emerson wrote that Thoreau "was ill and threatened with *lockjaw!* his brother's disease. It is strange—unaccountable—yet the symptoms seem precise and on the increase." Though the disease left after a while, its marks on Thoreau's psyche remained for a long time. According to one source it was years before he could speak of John's death without perceptible pain. In 1843 he became ill at least twice. Once it was apparently pulmonary weakness but in the other case it was probably because he had abandoned his beloved Concord for a term on Staten Island as a tutor. He himself called that illness unaccountable. Then came some years of better health. However, by the spring of 1855 he had contracted a lingering disorder from which he failed to recover until the summer of 1857. This siege too looks psychosomatic. Sometime after it started he wrote to H. G. O. Blake saying that he had been on his back for two or three months. He added, "I should feel a little less ashamed if I could give any name to my disorder, but I cannot, and our doctor cannot help me to it."

By the late 1850's he was alternating periods of health with growing periods of sickness. The most damaging blow to him before Brown's death was the death of John Thoreau, Sr. in February 1859. With his father dead Henry's Oedipal foe was gone. The son had triumphed, the mother was his. He had become head of the house and was responsible for conducting the family business as well. His feeling of guilt, though, at replacing his father must have been severe. His psyche now had suffered serious damage. His state of mind grew more and more depressed. He found some surcease in his writing and in the abolitionist movement but drew none from the family business and little from his friends. Brown's crusade jolted him out of himself for a time, giving him a cause to which he could dedicate his diminishing energies. There is an important if oblique statement to that effect in the *Journal* for October 22, 1859: "How many a man who was lately contemplating suicide has now something to live for!" But then came the crushing end to the crusade. As Ellery Channing recalled, "At the time of the John Brown tragedy, Thoreau was driven sick." Actually, it must have been the final blow to his spirit.

His end would not, however, come swiftly nor would his decline be steady. He would live for two years and some months more. Though I think that he soon realized he had no other recourse but death, I am sure that the will to die was not consistent. It waxed and waned. Thoreau could still write and talk even if the writing grew sluggish and the talk torpid. He could still show himself capable of indignation especially about the South and slavery. Yet gradually his fists unclenched. Returning to Concord in July 1861 after a futile trip to Minnesota for his health, he tried to go on his accustomed rounds. It was no use. By November he had written the last of the manifold pages of his Journal; by December he had taken to his bed. Nearing death he told Ellery Channing that he had no wish to live except for his mother and sister. "Some things must end," he observed significantly to Channing. But perhaps the most significant comment was made by a visitor to his bedside, Sam Staples. Sam, who was Thoreau's friend as well as his onetime jailer, spoke to Emerson about the visit. "Never spent an hour with more satisfaction," he said. "Never saw a man dying with so much pleasure and peace."

By the time he died he had already published his two best books, *A Week* and *Walden*. His most provocative essay, "Civil Disobedience," had reached print and so had the passionate polemics for John Brown. So had most of his poetry. After his death the finest of his nature essays appeared, essays better than anyone else could write, then or now. "Walking," "Autumnal Tints," "Wild Apples": each is an artist's and a naturalist's delight. Last came the travel books, edited for the most part by his surviving sister and Ellery Channing, *The Maine Woods, Cape Cod, A Yankee in Canada*. As public interest in Thoreau grew, much of his private writing was published, particularly the extensive Journal. In our time bits and pieces continue to appear, a little of the Journal for instance, some college essays, and a few other fugitive pages. There is more to be read yet but the best has been in print long enough to establish Thoreau as a writer whom the world would ignore only to its loss. And it is to understand Thoreau as a writer that we have speculated about his unconscious, theorized about his psychological problems. If our speculation seems forced, perhaps we can go back to the gentle, moderate way he himself once put it: "The poet cherishes his chagrins and sets his sighs to music."

# LUCKY FOX AT WALDEN

## C. ROLAND WAGNER

THOREAU WAS AN EARLY CONTRIBUTOR to the establishment of some of the central philosophical assumptions of our time. Initially and even finally an escapist, he yet laid down the pattern of a naturalistic world view which was to become part of the general conceptual framework of modern thought. In the work of such writers as Nietzsche, Conrad, Proust, Mann, Wallace Stevens and Santayana, we see the fuller realization of Thoreau's painful discoveries, his semi-articulated awareness of a world that had not yet been born. In the still "quiet sunshine of provincial prosperity" he began that terrible "blue voyage" from "conscience to consciousness" which has become the mark of the modern mind.

Our naturalistic world view, when fully articulated, contains at least three principles: the neutrality of nature, the savagery of human impulses disguised and checked by civilization, the idea of art as the mode of possible reconciliation. Thoreau advanced boldly on all these fronts; he saw clearly what more complex and subtle minds found impossible to see without irony, without insistence upon the legitimacy of the "opposing" point of view. He penetrated to fundamental truths with remarkable simplicity. Yet with all his courage he did not have the courage to accept what he himself began to articulate. His yearning for the infinite, for absolute union with something more than this world offers, fatally interfered. The transcendentalist in him—as still in so many today —prevented the naturalist from growing to maturity. Even at his best, in *Walden,* it is only (what William Drake calls) a "proto-naturalism" that emerges: the New Philosophy is intellectually outlined but is emotionally in doubt. And it is precisely Thoreau's irresolution about the meaning of nature that creates both the excitement and the final fuzziness of *Walden.*

Emotions, however, were indispensable to his intellectual conclusions. Confused idealism was the necessary (though not the sufficient) condition for Thoreau's apprehension of naturalistic truth. At first nature was regarded merely as more open, more available to spirituality, than society: nature does not take the narrowly moral point of view, it is not a mere reflection of the "jaundice" of man, it is not "petty" but "primeval" and "elemental." Thoreau was beginning to see nature apart from immediate human needs, but not apart from the ultimate human need for spiritual ecstasy. This is the emphasis in *A Week on the Concord and Merrimack Rivers* and in some of *Walden.* The viewpoint is summed up at the end of *A Week:* "Is not Nature, rightly read, that of which she is commonly taken to be the symbol merely?" Nature is not, as the other Transcendentalists were saying, the symbol of that "something more" to which we aspire, but is itself the answer to our dreams. Nature in her nakedness is what we want.

As Thoreau searched more deeply into the particulars of nature to find more intense and longer-lasting ecstasies, he began to notice the deep indifference, the utter irrelevance, of nature, not only to man's moral distinctions, but to his spiritual goal as well. Because it was impossible for him to remain satisfied with Emerson's belief that nature was "put forth" by an underlying Spirit, because he could not rest in any traditional form of pantheism, he began to recognize, although not to accept, the fact that nature had nothing to do with the final gratification he sought. He was forced to look at nature naturalistically, without illusion, as a clear-headed scientist would. This is the underlying theme of *Walden.* The only possible ecstasy suggested in that book, apart from momentary self-forgetfulness, is the ecstatic recognition of the truth of nature's indifference. Thoreau began his life with an infinite love and ended it in disintegration and unadmitted despair, but in between, in *Walden,* he glimpsed a world that might have been his.

That clear world transcends the Manicheanism of Melville and Hawthorne as well as the pantheism of Emerson and Whitman. Walden Pond is the place of mystery but, still more, the place of clarity and non-mythical truth. The inward reality it reflects is not infinitely mysterious, but like the pond itself is "a subject for the naturalist."

> It is remarkable how long men will believe in the bottomlessness of a pond without taking the trouble to sound it. . . . While men believe in the infinite some ponds will be thought to be bottomless. . . . [The] imagination, give it the least license, dives deeper and soars higher than Nature goes.

The imagination feeds on natural objects as representative of its inward rhythms but remains separate from those objects. In fact, it is the very neutrality of nature which makes possible its reflection of man. For nature, all the more "because she is not man," reflects him. Thus the receptive transparency of Walden makes possible the variety of its color:

> [It] is blue at one time and green at another, even from the same point of view. Lying between the earth and the heavens, it partakes of the color of both. . . . Yet a single glass of its water held up to the light is as colorless as an equal quantity of air.

But the implications of nature's neutrality go much further. Thoreau did not merely discover that external nature is indifferent, but that nature in *man* is indifferent to man's own "higher" goals. Like Hobbes and Spinoza, he discovered the non-rational wilderness in the human psyche which lies outside our moral judgments of good and evil—which is a mere fact to be grasped by the "naturalist." But unlike the earlier thinkers, and unlike anybody else before him that I know of, Thoreau discovered that neutral internal wilderness primarily *in himself,* existentially, and not merely in human nature around him. At the moral and imaginative center of *Walden,* at the beginning of the key chapter "Higher Laws," we find the following remarkable passage, one which has not gone unnoticed by critics, but whose full significance, I think, has not been appreciated:

> As I came home through the woods with my string of fish, trailing my pole, it being now quite dark, I caught a glimpse of a woodchuck stealing across my path, and felt a strange thrill of savage delight, and was strongly tempted to seize and devour him raw; not that I was hungry then, except for that wildness which he represented. Once or twice, however, while I lived at the pond, I found myself ranging the woods, like a half-starved hound, with a strange abandonment, seeking some kind of venison which I might devour, and no morsel could have been too savage for me. The wildest scenes had become unaccountably familiar. I found in myself, and still find, an instinct toward a higher, or, as it is named, spiritual life, as do most men, and another toward a primitive rank and savage one, and I reverence them both. I love the wild not less than the good.

The implications of this existential discovery, freed from Christian or any other traditional judgments of absolute value,[1] are not philosophically developed in *Walden,* or anywhere else in Thoreau's work, although there are innumerable paeans to wildness in all his writings. The confused remarks in "Higher Laws" that follow this clear and noble introductory statement betray Thoreau's ultimate failure to resolve the struggle between morality and nature. But no open confession of *final* failure is permitted. The next chapter, "Brute Neighbors," bounces back as though the confusions of "Higher Laws" do not exist, and shifts the main

---

[1] There is undoubtedly an unconscious element of romantic satanism here, a Baudelairian pleasure in the emotions of evil, but the predominant note is that of the naturalness of savage impulses and their relation to the inhuman savagery of the outer world of nature.

focus of attention from inwardness back to external nature again. Without explaining anything to the reader, without apology for his theoretical uncertainties, Thoreau employs nature to project a visionary or artistic solution to his dilemmas. It is as though he is saying: I cannot resolve my doubts about the wild and the good, the wilderness and civilization, but I can present my vision of what resolution might be.

The little introductory dialogue to "Brute Neighbors," imagined between the Hermit (Thoreau) and the Poet, bears out this interpretation. The somewhat heavy-handed humor reveals that Thoreau understands well enough the failure of "Higher Laws" to clarify the conflict between the transcendental and the natural: "Let me see, where was I? . . . Shall I go to heaven or a-fishing? . . . I was as near being resolved into the essence of things as ever I was in my life. I fear my thoughts will not come back to me. . . . What was it that I was thinking of? It was a very hazy day. . . . I know not whether it was the dumps or a budding ecstasy." He is more comfortable when he can look out to nature and find the objects suitable to his thought. How wonderful that his accidental surroundings should provide just the right ones!

> Why do precisely these objects which we behold make a world? Why has man just these species of animals for his neighbors; as if nothing but a mouse could have filled this crevice? I suspect that Pilpay & Co. have put animals to their best use, for they are all beasts of burden, in a sense, made to carry some portion of our thoughts.

These brute neighbors take their stand, like Thoreau himself, somewhere between civilization and the wilderness. Their savage impulses, directly satisfied, separated them from man's over-controlled world of "quiet desperation," yet they strangely remind us of human beings in their capacity to maintain their own kind of order in the midst of an indifferent nature. (At the same time, of course, Thoreau is suggesting how at home *he* is in the woods, since *he* is able to domesticate, temporarily at least, these wild creatures, or at least to feel comfortable with them.) The mouse that Thoreau plays "at bo-peep with" and feeds by holding "a piece of cheese between my thumb and finger" is a "wild native kind not found in the village." The young partridges blend easily into the environment, "often running their heads under a leaf" at "their mother's directions given from a distance, nor will your approach make them run again and betray themselves." Even when Thoreau holds them in his hand, "their only care, obedient to their mother and their instinct, was to squat there without fear or trembling." And so it is with many other half-wild and half-cultivated creatures of the nearby woods. They "live wild and free though secret in the woods, and still sustain themselves in the neighborhood of towns. . . . You only need sit still long enough in some attractive spot in the woods that its inhabitants may exhibit themselves to you by turns."

Even the war between the black ants and the red ants hints at possibilities for dialectical synthesis. The mock heroic style (and the size of the combatants) places the savagery at a distance, but the "microscope" Thoreau uses to observe the struggles of three particular ants brings it closer. He is both detached and involved, neutral with respect to the "issues," yet engaged by the human passions the battle symbolizes. Earlier, in the *Journal,* he confessed to "a deep sympathy with war, it so apes the gait and bearing of the soul"; now he finds that his feelings are "excited and harrowed by witnessing the struggle, the ferocity and carnage, of a human battle before my door."

He is fascinated by the ease with which a domesticated cat adjusts to life in the woods: ". . . by her sly and stealthy behavior proves herself more native there than the regular inhabitants." He recalls the so-called "winged-cat" that used to live near Walden several years before, speculating on its origins, and concluding that such a cat "would have been the right kind of cat for me to keep, if I had kept any; for why should not a poet's cat be winged as well as his horse?" Then, in the early fall, the loon arrives, its demoniacal laughter—"perhaps the wildest sound that is ever heard here"—and its capacity to outwit its pursuers reminding Thoreau of that wilderness that is beyond our capacity to control, that infinite dimension that never ceases to place all our finite adjustments in jeopardy. Summer and the illusion of final, safe, everlasting felicity are over. Yet the loon, within itself, apart from its relation to man, symbolizes that great elasticity in man, the power to touch both the depths and the heights of possible experience. For the loon both swims and flies: it swims confidently to great depths—"How surprised must the fishes be to see this ungainly visitor from another sphere speeding his way amid their schools!"—and it flies high enough to free itself temporarily from earthly attachments and still remain inside nature. Then, finally, the ducks come circling "round and round and over the pond at a considerable height, from which they could easily see to other ponds and the river, like black motes in the sky. . . ."

The abstract and concrete strands of Thoreau's vision of Walden are brought together in the penultimate chapter "Spring." He experiences the "inviolable health of nature" as a force transcending both ordinary love and ordinary disgust:

> . . . Nature is so rife with life that myriads can be afforded to be sacrificed and suffered to prey on one another; that

tender organizations can be so serenely squashed out of existence like pulp—tadpoles which herons gobble up, and tortoises and toads run over in the road; and that sometimes it has rained flesh and blood! . . . The impression made on a wise man is that of universal innocence. Poison is not poisonous after all, nor are any wounds fatal.

An innocence that is really earned comprehends both the momentary freedom which an indifferent nature may gratuitously permit —"Who knows what sort of seventeen-year locust will next come out of the ground?"—and acceptance of the eventual overthrow of all those conditions that make for freedom.

The work of art, which builds itself about those moments, celebrates a harmony, a liberation, entirely human, rooted in nature. "Be it life or death, we crave only reality." The life of art and the art of life are one. The conception of a perfected life in nature is identical with the conception of a perfected life in art. It involves the discovery that the spirit in man is a culmination and not a force, a result and not a cause, a kind of impotent alien in the very household of its earthly experiences. In part because Thoreau recognized that his yearning for absolute union could not be satisfied by nature, he paid close attention to the sense of "doubleness" in man, to that civilized "spectator" within which,

> as it were, is not a part of me, . . . sharing no experience, but taking note of it, and that is no more I than it is you. When the play, it may be the tragedy, of life is over, the spectator goes his way. It was a kind of fiction, a work of the imagination only, so far as he was concerned.

Like Proust, Wallace Stevens and Santayana, he saw that irrepressible realities can become airy nothings for the man of imagination, that life itself is the highest art for the disillusioned spirit, that "the language which all things and events speak" is finally a language "without metaphor, which alone is copious and standard."[2]

---

[2] "We seek / The poem of pure reality," writes Stevens, "untouched / By trope or deviation . . ."

> We seek
> Nothing beyond reality, Within it,
>
> Everything, the spirit's alchemicana
> Included, the spirit that goes roundabout
> And through included, not merely the visible,
>
> The solid, but the movable, the moment,
> The coming on of feasts and the habits of saints,
> The pattern of the heavens and high, night air.

## II

So much for that glimpse of a mature vision of the natural world and the possibilities of a liberated spirit. So much for what Santayana calls a two-story house of matter and spirit which, if it does not boast of ordinary living quarters between basement and attic, does rest on solid ground and does look out to a real world. Yet the real *Walden* as written is something else again. It is qualified by the vision but not dominated by it. It expresses the naturalistic possibility as well as the contradictory transcendental possibility, and fails to reconcile them, or fails to at least face up to the implications of the contradiction. That is why it seems to me misleading for critics to speak of the implicit dialectical structure of *Walden* without recognizing its failure to achieve dialectical synthesis. This is to confuse intention with realization.

It is true, as F. O. Matthiessen, Stanley Edgar Hyman, and Sherman Paul have indicated, that the structure of the work rests on the conception of a mythical or symbolic year underlying Thoreau's two and a half year experience at the pond. The seasons provide a framework within which the self can ritualize and dramatize its inward strivings and assist itself in transcending its own subjectivity. The central experience being celebrated is the rebirth of the natural man, the growth of the psyche from youth to maturity and back to youth again. The implication seems to be that an innocence that has grappled with experience is an earned innocence, that liberation from guilt is meaningful if one is willing to pay the price of confronting one's guilt. Although the first spring was not part of the "official" residence at Walden, which began on July 4th, and not in the proper order of the seasons that compose the symbolic year—which begins with Summer—its special function is to provide a standard of freedom, a golden beginning, like Proust's Combray, which must be (and implicitly has already been) recaptured by later maturity. As Sherman Paul writes:

> ... the first spring, the dewy, pure auroral season of the Olympian life, was true to his youth, and the subsequent seasons and the second spring were the record of the growth of consciousness and of his conscious endeavor to earn the new world of his springtime again.

But structure is one thing and fulfillment is another. It is one thing to discover that there is an underlying triadic movement from Purpose through Passion to Perception;[3] it is quite another to

---

[3] The terms come from *The Idea of a Theater* by Francis Fergusson and were adapted by Mr. Fergusson from Kenneth Burke's analysis of the tragic rhythm in *A Grammar of Motives.*

assert, as Mr. Hyman does, that this "vast rebirth ritual" is "the purest and most complete in our literature." Since Mr. Hyman would probably not agree with Richard Chase that there are "no sustained myths of initiation or of transfiguration in American literature," this is high praise indeed. Unfortunately, whenever we look beyond partial and isolated literary values, and beyond even an underlying sense of form, *Walden* fails to bring us that ripe clarification of experience which we ought to demand from all great writing.

We have already noted the philosophical confusion: Thoreau's Purpose was to penetrate the illusions of civilization to find spiritual truth in nature; his Passion was experiencing that higher truth symbolically only, within the compass of his imagination; his Perception *should have been* that there are no answers in nature, that the belief in ultimate meaning is itself an illusion. But although Thoreau does "perceive" that "Nature puts no questions and answers none which we mortals ask," he does not really accept the implications of his own perception. He does not see that he should be forced to reconstitute his quest for spiritual truth. In other words, although Thoreau, almost despite himself, *presents* the dialectic, he does not permit himself to *undergo* it. Like the ancient Stoics, and like his transcendental contemporaries, he could not admit to a fundamental disharmony between man and nature.

This can be substantiated more readily in the case of the *moral* (or mythic-moral) dialectic: Thoreau's Purpose was to break from the "traps" of civilization to find spiritual freedom; his Passion was experiencing a savagery that both promotes and endangers spirituality; his Perception *should have been* that the controls of civilization are essential to spiritual fulfillment. But we get from Thoreau only a grudging admission that civilization is important. "My house never pleased my eye so much after it was plastered, though I was obliged to confess that it was more comfortable." The emphasis in "House-Warming" (in which the retreat into the self-consciousness of Winter is represented) is much less on what is gained by maturity than on what must be given up to achieve it, much less on the advantages of facing the cold truth than on what Sherman Paul calls ". . . an estrangement from Nature, the sense of 'otherness' that bespoke his greatest loss."

And the estrangement is not really overcome in the final chapters. The reattachment to nature celebrated in "Spring" is not so fundamental as it tries to be, as it may initially appear to be, for it does not include as a felt part of the experience the tragic acceptance of civilized limitations on our deepest wishes. One triumphant symbol of renewal in "Spring," perhaps the central image of psychic fulfillment for Thoreau, is the unborn "graceful hawk"

—"Where was the parent which hatched it . . .?"—that appears "to have no companion in the universe,—sporting there alone,— and to need none but the morning and the ether with which it played."[4] The emphasis is still (although not entirely) on the childlike innocence that is supposed to have been dialectically transcended through the ritual cycle of the seasons.

But Thoreau really isn't committed to that hawk of pure nature either. Not only is a synthesis of nature and civilization beyond him; the rhythm of nature apart from civilization does not satisfy him either. R. W. B. Lewis believes that Thoreau reversed the traditional Christian idea of the sacrament by aiming to purify away, not the natural man of St. Paul but "the conventional or traditional man; in order, precisely, to bring into being the natural man." But if this is true, what is the meaning of the confused struggle in "Higher Laws" to purge away not only convention but nature herself?

> He is blessed who is assured that the animal is dying out in
> him day by day, and the divine being established. . . . Na-
> ture is hard to be overcome, but she must be overcome.

The truth is that Thoreau was up to his ears in St. Paul, that he was not only trying to purge away the guilt imposed by civilization, but *at the same time* maintaining and insisting on, and even extending, the sense of guilt to areas that few in the civilized world would concern themselves with. This was a man who was stimulated by the thought of the "marrow of koodoos devoured raw," who "could sometimes eat a fried rat with a good relish, if it were necessary," but who nevertheless could believe that "the imagination will not be reconciled to flesh and fat." "The wonder is how they, how you and I, can live this slimy, beastly life, eating and drinking."

The hawk, then, not only symbolizes the freedom of the natural man, but the freedom of the spiritual man as well. It represents both an escape from a supernatural morality and the reassertion of its necessity. The wild and the good are bound together in that hawk's eye of pure spirit in the manner of both Eastern and Western religions, contradicting Thoreau's own belief that nature is really enough for man. As a matter of fact, at the very time that he was revising *Walden* and beginning to use the cycle of the sea-

---

[4] I wonder how Mr. Hyman relates the hawk to what he calls "Thoreau's movement from an egocentric to a sociocentric view" of life? How sociocentric can a hawk get? (Perhaps Thoreau is thinking of the socially "responsible" Egyptian sun god Ra, symbolized by the hawk, or Horus, the hawk-headed god of day. But of course nothing of this is artistically realized in *Walden.*)

sons quite consciously as symbolic of the life of the spirit, he could not entirely commit himself to what he was doing. He was not altogether convinced that nature could even usefully *symbolize,* let alone embody, the ultimate quest of man. He wrote the following in his *Journal* for July 19, 1851:

> Here I am thirty-four years old, and yet my life is almost wholly unexpanded. . . . There is such an interval between my ideal and the actual in many instances that I may say I am unborn. . . . Methinks my seasons revolve more slowly than those of nature. . . . Is it important that I should mature as soon as an apple tree? Aye, as soon as an oak? May not my life in nature, in proportion as it is supernatural, be only the spring and infantile portion of my spirit's life? Shall I turn my spring to summer? May I not sacrifice a hasty and petty completeness here to entireness there? . . . My spirit's unfolding observes not the pace of nature. The society which I was made for is not here. Shall I, then, substitute for the anticipation of that this poor reality? I would [rather] have the unmixed expectation of that than this reality. . . .

And this was written by the same man who wrote: "Life or death, we crave nothing but reality!" I suppose one might attempt to force some kind of consistency into it. We might say that Thoreau sought to find spiritual emancipation through the cycle of nature, and that the culminating perception of the cycle was the recognition that his goal lay outside nature where the transcendental self would be reborn. But this idea is not embodied in any substantial way in *Walden;* in fact, as we have noted, it is mostly rejected. Both proto-naturalism on the one hand and a spirituality of the present moment on the other contradict this lingering supernaturalism. Thoreau could not contain them all within his art or his life.

### III

Perry Miller has written that the endless and "never quite definable fascination of *Walden*" lies in the author's sense of "doubleness," his awareness of the ambiguous relation between the natural and the spiritual; and that it was just this awareness and Thoreau's lack of capacity to live with it which finally "killed him." In order to understand how ideas can kill, in order to understand what Thoreau's philosophical conflicts meant to him, it is necessary to at least *suggest* a third approach to Thoreau—the psychoanalytical. Analysis in depth is certainly not popular with lovers of *Walden*— Raymond Gozzi's psychoanalytical study of Thoreau, "Tropes and Figures: A Psychological Study of David Henry Thoreau," an unpublished dissertation (New York University, 1957), sent shock waves of considerable force throughout the Thoreau Society and the Thoreau Society Bulletin—but it is useful for laying bare some of the enormous passions beneath the usually unruffled surface of this "bachelor of thought and Nature."

The structure as well as the major themes of *Walden* can, at least in part, be understood in terms of Thoreau's struggle for sexual identity. Without venturing too far outside *Walden* itself, except where doing so helps to substantiate what is already stated or implied there, we can say that Thoreau's central method for coping with his Oedipal wishes was unconsciously to submit to and unconsciously to avoid castration. The cycle of the seasons was chosen as the basic structure of *Walden* to allay the castration anxiety of a man who saw in nature the symbols of fulfillment with Mother.

In *A Week on the Concord and Merrimack Rivers* (most of which was written during the ecstatic period while Thoreau was living at Walden) there was not yet any major concern to allay castration anxiety. In that book Thoreau had already moved away from the idea of nature as a symbol of a higher (theistic) world, had already begun to question the idea of nature as a symbol of a deeper (transcendental) world, and was then considering the possibility that nature herself is the ideal we are searching for. ("Is not Nature, rightly read, that of which she is commonly taken to be the symbol merely?") The joy of passive receptivity, of identification with the Mother within himself was dominant. Our birth, he writes, creates a wound in nature ("our mother"), and not till the wound heals and the scar disappears do we begin to discover where we are, and that nature is one and continuous everywhere." In the ecstatic moments celebrated in *A Week,* in the hymn to an ideal homoerotic Friendship, in the passive opening of himself to influences of morning, noon and night, in the rejection of the literal truth of the masculine God of Christianity, Thoreau expressed the temporary re-establishment of that unconscious continuity with Mother that was sundered by birth.

In *A Week* he did not need to be especially anxious about his masculine identity because he had, in effect, freely abandoned it. He had symbolically castrated himself and was reaping the advantages of castration without yet being concerned with its disadvantages. The conclusion of the book is a prose hymn to Solitude and Silence, a devotional, as it were, to emasculation. How wonderful that the pursuit of Sound and Meaning issues finally in the reception of a Soundlessness beyond meaning! "It were vain for me to endeavor to interpret the Silence. She cannot be done into English." Mother nature can be experienced by her worshipper but not understood, "for when he at length dives into her, so vast is the disproportion of the told to the untold that the former will seem but the bubble on the surface where he disappeared."

The temporary gain achieved was symbolic sexual union with Mother without fear of castration by Father. By becoming *like* Mother he could perhaps *have* Mother without fear of Father.[5] If the sexual organ is deposited in nature and then abandoned, clearly one need not be afraid of having it removed. If one gives one's property away it can no longer be stolen. The unconscious game continued in *Walden* but with a difference. Thoreau now anxiously *insists* on the advantages of castration and *protests* that there are no disadvantages. The free and easy attitude of *A Week* is gone. Not only can we gain the ecstasy of ultimate union, he implies, but we are all the more masculine for giving up the social trappings of masculine power. Ordinary folks are "emasculated by luxury," he writes, while the superior man is capable of a "voluntary poverty"; his "chastity" is his potency. How much better to be alone and independent than together and dependent. Even those who have plumed themselves on their individuality are suspect. "The success of great scholars and thinkers is commonly a courtier-like success, not kingly, not manly. They make shift to live merely by conformity, practically as their fathers did, and are in no sense the progenitors of a nobler race of men." "Conformity," of course, is feminine, signifies dependence, and dependence for Thoreau is essential weakness. "I have lived some thirty years on this planet, and I have yet to hear the first syllable of valuable or even earnest advice from my seniors. . . . If I have any experience which I think valuable, I am sure to reflect that this my Mentors said nothing about."

Thoreau is proud to "purify" himself of worldly attachments: ". . . I never got my fingers burned by actual possession." He builds his house alone, with little indirect help, satisfies his hunger with a handful of huckleberries, and suggests how much wiser and stronger he is than poor John Field, because, unlike that "honest, hard-working, but shiftless" Irish family man, he "did not use tea, nor coffee, nor butter, nor milk, nor fresh meat, and so did not have to work to get them. . . ." It may be superficially true, as Sherman Paul insists, answering Emerson's criticism of Thoreau's rigid stoicism, that "the renunciations of wife, taxes, church, vote, meat, wine, and tobacco" were hardly "losses compared to what Thoreau gained." But what did these worldly interests *signify* to Thoreau? Were they not much more than separate, calculable,

---

[5] Identification and object choice, normally independent mechanisms, were here combined, and identification became a means for maintaining possession of the chosen object. Cf. Freud, *New Introductory Lectures* (New York, 1933), p. 91.

hedonistic elements to be mathematically weighed against other "spiritual" satisfactions? Were they not expressions of the whole sphere of masculine power and responsibility? Emerson properly sensed that Thoreau's sacrifices distorted the character of whatever he gained. Some of our more sympathetic modern critics too easily accept Thoreau's own word that he got what he wanted, at least temporarily, from his life in nature. He may be able to convince his more worshipful readers of his calm confidence when he insists that he "can sit and . . . stand without the aid of a furniture warehouse," but what do these readers do when the enormity of Thoreau's sacrifice is suddenly revealed in brilliant but nevertheless psychologically transparent images?

He was a lucky fox that left his tail in the trap. The muskrat will gnaw his third leg off to be free.

Even self-mutilation can be turned into art. "When I think of the muskrat," he writes in the *Journal,* "gnawing off his leg, it is as the plectrum on the harp or the bow upon the viol, drawing forth a majestic strain or psalm, which immeasurably dignifies our common fate."

If civilization is a "trap" for Thoreau from which he can escape only by sacrificing his manhood, the music of that escape, the celebration of spiritual "victory," can be little more than a beautiful wish-fulfillment. To a remarkable extent, in fact, the whole of *Walden* is such a wish-fulfillment, a way of making up for a terrible sense of loss, a way of easing the anxiety of a tail left in the trap, of a gnawed off third leg—how does Thoreau know which is the third leg? We have already noted Thoreau's own confession of severe doubt about even the *symbolic* usefulness of the cycle of the seasons. I would now suggest that the deepest reason for that doubt is that he could not resolve his incestuous longings in a civilized way and so was unable to ease the increasing castration anxiety that overcame him after his two year experiment in the woods. The basic structure of *Walden* (as J. Lyndon Shanley has proved) developed after the Walden period, and was an attempt to come to terms with the unconscious problems that arose in Thoreau's mind in reflecting upon the original experience. The ritual of rebirth was chosen in the hope that his masculine identity would necessarily be renewed with the Spring after his Winter of loss and discontent.

The triadic rhythm of conscious experience in *Walden* has its parallels in unconscious experience. Consciously Thoreau aimed to escape the "rotten" family life of the civilized world, the incestuously "bad air" of the houses of Concord, and find purity; unconsciously (like Oedipus, when he left the home of his supposed parents to avoid his fate) his Purpose was to pursue the same "rotten" end. Consciously Thoreau was overwhelmed by his own ineluctable impurity—"The wonder is how they, how you and I, can live this slimy, beastly life, eating and drinking"; unconsciously his Passion was a severe attack of castration anxiety. Consciously he tried to resolve the opposition between his sense of purity and impurity by reattaching himself to a more comprehensive idea of nature; unconsciously his Perception was that he did not need to feel castrated, that the return of Spring guaranteed his wholeness, that he who hath abandoned house, brethren, sisters, father, mother, wife, children, and lands for the higher good shall receive back all these things, *without* persecutions, and in *this* world, eternal life.

But the Perception was not much more than a wish-fulfillment. Thoreau could not really sustain belief in his own masculine identity. He could only insist on it. He could only ritually and aggressively repeat that he was reconciled to the real world beyond purity and impurity. His demand for purity could not be satisfied; and that demand, together with anger at the world for not satisfying it, determine much of both the form and the content of *Walden,* and prevent it from being *finally* more than an infantile response to experience. Still, an ironic reserve, a partial recognition of the dialectic of the wilderness and civilization, keeps *Walden* within the confines of rational discourse. It is in his political essays that the infantile wishes begin to escape all civilized limits. There Thoreau's struggle for inward identity, his rage against the ideas of passive submission and apparently arbitrary authority, almost makes him lose contact with the real world and express his fantasies only.

Heinz Eulau has shown how morally and politically naive Thoreau's three major essays on political questions are. Associating the character of each essay with the changing tenor of Thoreau's humor, Mr. Eulau writes that "Civil Disobedience," the earliest essay, at best creates an atmosphere of mischief ". . . more literary than political" in which the real problem of slavery becomes insignificant in comparison to Thoreau's adolescent war with all civilized authority; "Slavery in Massachusetts" is "scornful and vitriolic," advocating secession for Massachusetts without any awareness "that the consequences of such action might accentuate the evil which Thoreau sought to remedy"; finally, "A Plea for Captain John Brown," in which humor gives way to "blasphemy," expresses Thoreau's views "unequivocally," according to Mr. Eulau, revealing that Thoreau's "mind was totally closed to the democratic conception of politics as a never-ending process of compromise and adjustment."

Thoreau's uncompromising moral idealism, despite its occasional embodiment in sentences of supreme literary power,[6] created an essentially child's view of political and social reality. Because his moral principles were little more than expressions of his quest for purity and of hostility to any civilized interference with the absolute attainment of his wishes, he was unable to discriminate between better and worse in the real world. "The only obligation which I have a right to assume is to do at any time what I think right." And what he thought "right" was not so much the reduction of human exploitation in real social situations as the manumission of that invisible black man, Henry David, to permit him to gratify his irresponsible desires. Thoreau "democratically" sympathizes with nameless ordinary folk when he thinks of them as outsiders, unwilling victims of the hated social authority; he despises the same folk when he thinks of them as obedient to authority or as weak victims of the industrial world. He never specifically relates these ambivalent attitudes to the lives of actual people because *he* is both slave and slaveowner, *he* is ambivalently involved in both passivity and dominance, *his* "thoughts are murder to the State" and to himself.

"A Plea for Captain John Brown" expresses these conflicting feelings with little disguise—too little for civilized discourse. This remarkable essay was delivered as a speech in 1859, a few months after the death of Thoreau's father. Its description of Brown tells us as much about Thoreau as it does about Brown—both what he *thought* he (Thoreau) was and, to some extent, what he really was. The hard romantic from Concord identified with the "heroic" Puritan Brown, who seemed to combine the virtues of the dreamer and the man of action.

> He was a man of Spartan habits, and at sixty was scrupulous about his diet at your table, excusing himself by saying that he must eat sparingly and fare hard, as became a soldier or one who was fitting himself for difficult enterprises, a life of exposure. . . . [He] referred to what his family had suffered in Kansas, without ever giving the least vent to his pent-up fire. It was a volcano with an ordinary chimney-flue.

He ridicules the idea that Brown was insane:

> Insane! A father and six sons, and one son-in-law, and several more men besides,—as many at least as twelve disciples,—all struck with insanity at once; while the sane

---

[6] For example: "Surely they [John Brown and his followers] were the very best men you could select to be hung. That was the greatest compliment which this country could pay them. They were ripe for her gallows."

tyrant holds with a firmer grip than ever his four millions of slaves, and a thousand sane editors, his abettors, are saving their country and their bacon! ... Do the thousands who know him best, who have rejoiced at his deeds in Kansas, and have afforded him material aid there, think him insane? Such a use of this word is a mere trope with most who persist in using it. ...

Gilman Ostrander believes that Thoreau and Emerson failed to understand Brown primarily because Brown did not confess the whole terrible truth about his Kansas campaigns when he spoke to them earlier in Massachusetts. "[They] assumed that if his character could be proved to be pure, it would follow that his actions must have been justified." But for Thoreau, at least, the issue was more complex. Granted that he would have been shocked if he knew the entire truth about Brown, it is nevertheless the case that moral purity and the imagination of violence went together for Thoreau; and not merely because violence *in this instance* might rationally be justified to support the life of principle, nor even only, as Mr. Eulau believes, because of a disguised expediency principle that any means could be justified by a good end, but *essentially* because purity required the imagination of violence. The need for violence came first, the good end second; violence had to find the good end to justify itself. John Brown expressed publicly what Thoreau felt privately. Brown did not merely reverence the idea of a "wildness whose glance no civilization can endure"; he did not merely desire to eat a woodchuck raw: he really ate the woodchuck.

Thoreau was not insane and Brown probably was, yet Thoreau grasped Brown's character well enough to understand how Brown could justify violence in the name of absolute principle. But it was an unconscious understanding. Thoreau sensed that Brown killed the representatives of civilized authority in part because they were simply authorities and had to be destroyed. (As Mr. Eulau writes: "[Thoreau] confused what seemed to him the iniquity of law with the legal process itself.") But Brown had to be destroyed too: "I see now that it was necessary that the bravest and humanest man in all the country should be hung." Perhaps this is no more than to suggest that the country was so evil that crucifixion was essential for any ultimate good to come from Brown's violence. But a moment later he hints at something more:

I *almost fear* that I may yet hear of his deliverance, doubting if a prolonged life, if any life can do as much good as his death.

Is it possible that we are also being told that, because Thoreau shares in those crimes of violence, both he and Brown have to pay for them, that they must both be punished? Is the "secret sharer" of Brown's terrible inner life at the edge of a confession? Perhaps Brown must be crucified because he killed the Father: he must take all the sins of Walden Pond upon his shoulders.

Brown was a monstrous mirror of Thoreau's inner life, reflecting all the damned up wildness of a male Hester Prynne—but he was *no more* than a mirror to Thoreau, not a real person to be rationally and sympathetically understood. Thoreau did not understand Brown nor, apparently, anybody else as "simple separate" persons distinct from himself. He had no real sense of other people; he penetrated to great depths but overlooked the intervening reality. He omitted what Mr. Krutch calls the "middling concerns" between the "primitive and the ineffable." His "great fault," said Whitman, "was disdain—disdain for men (for Tom, Dick and Harry): inability to appreciate the average life— even the exceptional life: it seemed to me a want of imagination. He couldn't put his life into any other life—realize why one man was so and another man was not so. . . ." He sacrificed a portion of the human in order to make contact with what he thought super-human and sub-human. He was what John Stuart Mill, in discussing Bentham, describes as a "one-eyed man" in both his failure and his success.

> For our own part, we have a large tolerance for one-eyed men, provided their one eye is a penetrating one: if they saw more, they probably would not see so keenly, nor so eagerly pursue one course of inquiry.

# THOREAU AND JOHN BROWN

## TRUMAN NELSON

THE ACCURSED QUESTION in Thoreau's day, that issue that every man in his time has to make a choice of confronting, or going around, was the peculiar institution of chattel slavery. The personality in which the resistance to it was most perfectly seated was John Brown, the first white American to attack slavery with force and violence on the soil where it existed and with a combined armed group of black men and whites. He went up against this tyranny so that it had to give way to him or he to it, and this, as Thoreau pointed out, "distinguished him from every other reformer I know."

In the midst of the shock waves from Harper's Ferry, a lurid drama which affected the whole American people in the same way the performance of a ritual tragedy used to purge, with pity and with fear, the citizens of Athens, Thoreau also distinguished himself from all other reformers by speaking out in Brown's defense. The chronology of his stand is highly significant. It took place *before* Brown had had his day in court and had aroused the country with that great affirmation of his purpose and character which, like an unexpected flash of summer lightning, made incandescent the acts, meditations and resolves that summed up the totality of his life . . . and inevitably made his death a martyrdom.

As Thoreau spoke, the Republican Party, staking its future on a policy of slavery containment, vociferously condemned the deed. The *Liberator,* after thrumming incessantly for over a quarter of a century that the slave must be free, called it a misguided, wild and insane effort. On all sides the most liberal people were drawing aside in holy horror, declaring they hadn't done it, or countenanced him to do it, in any conceivable way. "You needn't take so much pains to wash your skirts of him," Thoreau said. "No intelligent man will ever be convinced that he was any creature of yours." But even Brown's best friends murmured that the old man was a little unhinged on the subject of slavery.

Immediately after the sensational and distorted reports of the raid filled the papers, Thoreau's *Journal* began to blaze with anger over the abuse and defamation poured from all quarters on John Brown. He told himself, and later some others, that he knew a little about Captain Brown and that he wanted to correct the tone and the errors in the press and on the lips of his neighbors and countrymen respecting the Captain's character and action. "It costs us nothing to be just," he said. "We can at least express our sympathy with, and admiration of, him and his companions, and that is what I now propose to do. . . . As for his recent failure," he added, truthfully, a little later, "We do not know the facts about it."

The cost of justice to others was not then so high as it is now, with our new concept of guilt by association, but I imagine there are still a few men around who would do the same today for someone in a similar plight . . . defend a man's *character* against common accusations without knowing the *facts*. It was a temperate and fair-minded statement of purpose, but this temperance did not long continue. A few paragraphs later he was proclaiming that the event was a touchstone bringing out with glaring distinctness the character of the government. "I see now it was necessary that the bravest and humanest man in all the country should be hung. If any leniency were shown him, any compromise made with him, any treating with him at all, he might be suspected. And furthermore I rejoice that I live in this age, that I am his contemporary . . . and all in all, it is the best news I ever had."

This is most curious for a man who did not know the facts, a man who had scarcely been known to praise another human being before. Who had spent a lifetime observing with meticulous accuracy the life cycle of a leaf. Who would squat, patient and immobile for hours, to shake hands with a woodchuck. Is it not curious that this fastidious and accurate man should say these things of a man in chains and self-condemned of treason and murder . . . or at least, of killing? If there are any doubts that Thoreau rejected non-resistance and even passive resistance, his position toward John Brown has blasted them forever.

Millions of toiling graduate students have speculated on what Thoreau meant when he said he had lost a hound, a bay horse and a turtledove. There has been little speculation on what is a real mystery, in the light of contemporary value judgments: his considered opinion of John Brown as "a man of rare common sense and directness of speech, as of action, a transcendentalist above all, a man of ideas and principles . . . that was what distinguished him. Not yielding to a whim or transient impulse but carrying out the purpose of a life." How does this square with the Emersonian definitions, or non-definitions, of Transcendentalism in which this revolutionary theology appears somewhat as a "saturnalia of whim," impulse, and the purest individualism?

In many ways, the best description of Henry Thoreau comes in Emerson's marvelously perceptive lecture on Transcendentalism in 1842. I think it really *made* Thoreau. It was nature imitating art. Emerson described the Transcendentalist as believing, first of all, "You may think me a child of circumstances: I make my own circumstance." The perfectibility of man becomes the perfectibility of me. The Transcendentalist is lonely, he shuns society as imperfect, as evil. "He whoso goes to walk alone, accuses the world." Unlike John Brown, he never plans. Everything has to be instinctive and new. "I do not wish to do one thing but once. I do not love routine."

But when he does act, that action can be revolutionary. To illustrate this, Emerson quotes Jacobi, who: "would assassinate like Timoleon; would perjure myself like Epaminondas and John de Witt. I would resolve on suicide like Cato; I would commit sacrilege with David; yea, and pluck corn of the Sabbath, for no other reason than that I was suffering from lack of food. For I have assurance in myself, that, in pardoning those faults according to the letter, man exerts the sovereign rights which the majesty of his being confers on him."

With this sort of eloquence and self-deception, Transcendentalism conferred on individualism a morality it did not deserve. For every action based on one man's "sovereign rights" is bound to debase the sovereign rights of another man. Actually, very few Transcendentalists ever acted at all, and this is the reason why they did not: because they knew *all* acts are invasive of others. If they did, sooner or later they had a failure of nerve, and without a real plan which had allowed for this invasion and its reaction, their acts became an exercise in futility. Finally, in combat with slavery, they learned to organize and plan, instead of going by Christ's rule to take no thought for the morrow. They began to realize that Transcendentalism could be more than an exalted private whim, could become a very pure and optative recognition of the highest human potential. Or, as the brilliant modern philosopher Herbert Marcuse put it, in his *One Dimensional Man,* Transcendentalism designates "tendencies in theory and practice which in a given society, 'overshoot' the established universe of discourse and action toward its historical alternatives (real possibilities)."

It was the problem of reaction to the invasion of persons that the Transcendentalist had to face in their assessment of John Brown. Brown tried to get people to do what they did not want to do. They fought back and he killed them. Transcendentalism in theory had such respect for the private character of man it would hardly judge him at all, let alone condemn him to death. Transcendentalism, like pure pacifism, was theoretically based on the supreme dignity of the individual man, which included the supreme inviolability of his body against the physical invasion of bloodletting.

"John Brown," says one of the most noted of modern historians, Allen Nevins, doubtlessly speaking for the majority of his fellows, "was an ignorant, narrowminded, thoroughly selfish egotist, with a vein of hard cruelty and was in fact, insane and fanatically prejudiced, a religious maniac."

"John Brown," said one of his contemporaries many years afterwards in the New York *Sun,* "in Kansas, at Pottawatomie, dragged from their beds at midnight, three men and two boys and hacked them in pieces with two-edged cleavers in such a way that the massacre was reported to be the work of wild animals. If any butcher in New York should hack and slash his own hogs and steers as this man hacked to death these two boys, he would be arrested and imprisoned without delay."

All these things were said, and much worse . . . that he was at Harper's Ferry to touch off a massive slave insurrection in which every white man, woman and child in the slave country would be in imminent danger of being butchered in the night, in their beds . . . all these horrible things were being written about John Brown at the precise time Thoreau was saying no man in America had ever stood up so persistently and effectively for the dignity of human nature. "I read all the newspapers I could within a week after the event," he said, "and I do not remember a single expression of sympathy for the seventeen white men and five Negroes concerned in the enterprise."

He was the first. Then Emerson said the gallows holding John Brown would become a cross. Then Theodore Parker wrote from Italy that "A man held against his will as a slave has a natural right to kill everyone who seeks to prevent his enjoyment of liberty. . . . A freeman has a natural right to help the slaves recover their liberty, and in that enterprise to do for them, all which they have a right to do for themselves. . . . It may be a natural duty for the freeman to help the slaves to the enjoyment of their liberty, and as means to that end, to aid them in killing all such as oppose their natural freedom."

Parker was a blunter man than Thoreau, and besides he was out of the country, dying in Rome. But could not Thoreau have been in agreement with Parker's revolutionary affirmations? Horace Greeley, in printing Thoreau's incendiary speech (made in Framingham at the time Garrison, on the platform with him, burned the Constitution on a pewter plate) called Thoreau the country's greatest champion of the natural law philosophy, placing him above Sumner, Seward and Chase in this respect. But after Harper's Ferry Greeley had great reservations about natural law in the revolutionary context and said Brown was wrong and the freeing of the slave could come about more quickly and decently by "the quiet diffusion of the sentiments of humanity" without any "outbreak."

How Thoreau pours scorn on this liberalism. "The slave ship is on her way, crowded with its dying victims; new cargoes are being added in mid ocean; a small crew of slaveholders, countenanced by a large body of passengers, is smothering four millions under the hatches, and yet the politician asserts that the only proper way by which deliverance is to be obtained, is by 'the quiet diffusion of the sentiments of humanity' without any 'outbreak.' As if the sentiments of humanity were ever found unaccompanied by its deeds, and you could disperse them all finished to order, the pure article, as easily as water with a watering-pot and so lay the dust. What is that that I hear cast overboard? The bodies of the dead that have found deliverance. This is the way we are 'diffusing' humanity and its sentiments with it."

This is an outcry for the deed, for the revolutionary act. And this is not the first time he did this. I could never understand how writing as full of revolutionary incitements as "Civil Disobedience" can be fed like pap to students without, until recently, causing any noticeable upheavals. It clearly teaches the overthrow of the government. It is subversive under all the present definitions of that very elastic impugnment. He says, "all men recognize the right of revolution" and then adds, "When a sixth of the population which has undertaken to be the refuge of liberty are slaves and a whole country is unjustly overrun and conquered by a foreign army and subjected to military law, I think that it is not too soon for honest men to rebel and revolutionize. What makes this duty the more urgent is the fact that the country so overrun is not ours, but ours is the invading army." What would happen if Thoreau said this today at a Vietnam teach-in? He leaves none of the sacred cows unscathed in "Civil Disobedience," giving a death wound to the democratic process itself. . . . "All voting is a sort of gaming, like checkers or backgammon. . . ."

But something in this essay took the revolutionary edge off it. Its underlying anarchy, perhaps, and individualism. It is so patently a call for individuals to be more so: not to unite against a common enemy with a common program, which is a dangerous thought, but to strive so as to get the State to recognize "the individual as a higher and independent power." But what individual? What *kind* of individual? One can be an individual like John Bunyan and sit in jail for acting against the state and write *Pilgrim's Progress*. Or like Hitler and write *Mein Kampf*. One can be a radical, a severe critic of the status quo in the context of individualism, but you cannot be a revolutionary without connections with like-minded dissenters in the mass, wherever they are in upheaval, and fighting in line with them.

Thoreau submitted meekly to the force used by Sam Staples in placing him under lock and key in Concord Jail. There is no recorded outcry. He sat at the barred window listening to the voices of his townsmen, heard clearer than he had ever heard them before. He called to none of them to rescue him. He felt no resentment against Staples, who was acting according to his individual belief. And when he got out in the morning, it was because, as he complained, "someone interfered," and paid the tax. He had performed an act of defiance as an individualist: leaving others to join him or not at the prompting of their individual conscience, or their inner light. There was no reason, he felt, for him to do as his neighbors did, but by the same token, there was reason for them to do what he did. Thus principle is canceled out. So he remained, in his first encounter with the accursed question, the completely self-orbed transcendentalist-individualist, marching to the drum he heard, in the direction his inner self laid out. And if your drum beat leads you up against the State, do not step aside, the monster can only block your body, your senses. Let them lock the door on you if they will, your thoughts will go marching on, and they are really all that is dangerous.

In his next great polemic, spoken at the Anti-Slavery meeting at Framingham, July 4th, 1854, he shows, I feel, profound revolutionary growth. He sees now that it is not only the uniformed and formal state which functions as a repressive force, but that the church and press act upon our minds in the same way the state confronts our bodies. Twelve Massachusetts men were in jail in Boston for attempting to rescue a slave, Anthony Burns, on the eve of his return to his master in Virginia under the terms of the Fugitive Slave Law. These men, incited by Wendell Phillips, Theodore Parker and Samuel Gridley Howe, and led by Thomas Wentworth Higginson (who escaped arrest) had broken down the door of the Boston Courthouse where the slave was confined and had then been driven off by deputy sheriffs. One of the deputies was killed. The men, five of them Negroes, were accused of murder, or arrested for murder. The grand jury had not yet indicted them. They had acted.

American historiography has been so adept in recent years, in cutting our sinews to our own revolutionary past, and the New Critics so successful in exorcising every vestige of "statement" and politics from our "literature," that not one reader in a thousand knows what Thoreau was actually talking about in his Framingham Speech, aptly titled "Slavery in Massachusetts." Thoreau was angry; he was intemperately furious because the twelve men who had tried to rescue the slave with axes and meat cleavers were still in a Massachusetts jail and no one was trying to get them out. This is what he meant by *Slavery in Massachusetts!* All the Massachusetts liberals wanted to talk about was something happening a thousand miles off in Kansas. Thoreau compared the assault on the courthouse to the action at Lexington Green.

Instead, this time, of being anti-state, he complains that although he had read recently of a state law making it a crime for any officer of the state to detain a fugitive slave, this law had been broken. And although a writ of replevin had been secured by the slave's sympathisers which could have legally taken him from the custody of the Federal Marshal, it "could not be served, for want of sufficient force to aid the officer." He castigates the Governor for not supplying this force. Was that not his duty as the executive officer of the State? He is useless, or worse than useless then, if he permits the law to go unexecuted. Thoreau is now *for* the law, for its physical enforcement at the point of a gun. What was wrong was that the State put its military force into the service of the slaveholder and the Federal Government! He asks indignantly why Massachusetts has been training these soldiers in the arts of violence if they cannot save a citizen of Massachusetts from being kidnapped? Thus, militarism itself is permissible if used for a purpose of which Thoreau approves.

As for individualism, this time he would rather trust to the "united sentiment of the people"; the judge could decide this way or that, his opinion was only "the trammelled judgement of an individual, of no significance, be it which way it might." In fact, the people, *en masse,* should go behind the courts, as the imprisoned twelve did, for "the law will never make me free, it is men who have got to make the law free. They are lovers of law and order, who observe the law when the government breaks it."

Thoreau was speaking here of a specific law, not some vague concept of "natural law." He was saying that the Federal Government had no right to enforce the Fugitive Slave Law against a state statute restricting it and that the men attacking the courthouse were carrying out a proper function of the Massachusetts government. He then offered a concrete program, not for individualists, because it strikes directly at the right of private judgment, editorially speaking. "Among measures to be adopted, I would suggest to make as earnest and vigorous an assault on the press as had already been made, and with effect, on the church." What happens here to the infinitudes of the private man? As a preacher? As an editor? He is a dead duck. "The freemen of New England have only to refrain from purchasing and reading these sheets, have only to withhold their cents, to kill a score of them at once." The editors have kept step with the wrong drum. He feels that editors and preachers, as well as politicians, are wrong because they are totally concerned with "the mismanagement of wood, and iron and stone." And that in combination they act upon the consciousness of the people of Massachusetts until they are brought ignobly to say, "Do what you will, O Government, with my wife and children, my mother and brother, my father and sister, I will obey your commands to the letter."

Thoreau in 1861, age 44, a year before his death · from an ambrotype by E. S. Dunshee
*courtesy of Concord Free Public Library · photo by Keith Martin, Concord*

Thoreau's cabin at Walden · pencil drawing by MAY ALCOTT, published 1869
*courtesy of Fruitlands Museum · photo by Shaw Studios, Boston*

Against this stultification, this moral paralysis, this slavery, Thoreau utters one of the most violent statements ever written, or spoken before a mass audience: "Rather than do this, I need not say what match I would touch, what system endeavor to blow up but as I love my life, I would side with the light, and let the dark earth roll from under me, calling my mother and brother to follow."

There is no telling what would have happened to Thoreau as a writer and as a man if he had been approached directly after his inflammatory speech by some of the breed of youth we see around today on picket lines, sit-ins, sleep-ins, teach-ins, or traveling perilously to Mississippi or Cuba. If some of these, in the blue jeans and sneakers of that day had come and said, "Like man we want to enforce the law when the government breaks it," he might have been, in the realm of action, much more than Captain of a Huckleberry Party. At least, for once, he would have had a direct reply to one of his rare collective proposals.

But no answer came to his "Slavery in Massachusetts," and this element of failure must be taken into consideration in explaining some of the misanthropy of the later years. He was always unlucky in his audiences. . . . "Civil Disobedience" ended up in the quietest category of "Aesthetic Papers," and the people he was agitating in Framingham were devout pacifists of the Garrison school, themselves locked in the violence versus non-violence dilemma plaguing and, I feel, paralysing the civil rights movement today. No one of these had any cannon fuses for him to touch a match to, or any bombs for him to throw. As far as any practical purpose was concerned, their attitudes were as inert and gradual as the politicians who felt that they could redeem the slave ship with its hideous cargo with the oil of compromise and the winds of constitutional prose.

Again and again, after the Anthony Burns case in 1854, the North, largely against "slavery in the abstract," went down to defeat when pitted against the simple-minded racism of the white South. This plunged Thoreau further into a long period of discouragement and despair. He became so weary of the confusion and ineptness of the Northern role in Kansas, and of the American liberal, seized, as ever, by a paralysis of motion in the face of a vast moral problem demanding immediate and drastic action, that he wrote in his *Journal,* "only absorbing employment prevails, succeeds, drives Kansas out of your head. The attitude of resistance is one of weakness, in as much as it only faces an enemy, it has its back to all that is truly attractive."

This sort of comment is generally taken as proof that Thoreau was never aligned with the real radicals and was a writer at heart and nothing but a writer. But its shocking polar bleakness could only come in a great pendulum-like swing from a heart packed with fiery heat over the sins and failures of his society. There are few evidences in literature of a stronger social agony than in the outcry of the shy little man in the green groves of Framingham about the match he would touch, the system he would blow up . . . a statement so outrageous that generally speaking only the most callous demagogue would say it in public, if at all.

His state of mind at this time is clearly revealed in a letter to his English friend, Thomas Cholmondeley. "There has not been anything which you could call union between the North and South in this country for many years, and there cannot be so long as slavery is in the way. I only wish the Northern . . . that any men . . . were better material, or that I for one had more skill to deal with them: that the North had more spirit and would settle the question at once, and here instead of struggling feebly and protractedly away off on the plains of Kansas." In another paragraph Thoreau writes: "I dwell as much aloof from society as ever: find it just as impossible to agree in opinion with the most intelligent of my neighbors."

Here is Thoreau's fatal contradiction full blown. In one vein he wants to arouse, he wants to lead, he wants to help settle the great struggle of his time, by force if necessary, and in the other he proclaims himself an avowed recluse, unable to share a common opinion with anyone. He had become the revolutionary *manqué,* completely at odds with the society around him. But he could not seem to go beyond this. On one hand he was deeply aware of the struggle between will and duty which takes place in the consciousness of the artist who wants to create something incarnate in himself, but is drawn into a common struggle in which he has to be *selfless.* Every writer knows this: if you surrender your being to a Cause, you can't write for a while. Not the way you want to, out of your deepest self. On the other his anger and frustration at the defeat of the Free State elements in Kansas were so acute that he was using his work as a secondary motive, as therapy, which is also fatal to the self-infatuation that high creativity demands. "Only absorbing employment prevails," he says, "drives Kansas out of your head."

His perceptive friend Cholmondeley seemed to feel that the collective, or the *societal* side of Thoreau was struggling for expression. "You are not living together as I could wish," he replied. "You ought to have society. You should be a member of a society not yet formed. You want it greatly and without this you will be liable to moulder away as you get older. . . . Your love for, and intimate acquaintance with, Nature is ancillary to some affection which you have not yet discovered . . . take up every man as you would take up a leaf, and look attentively at him."

Thoreau had already tried this and it had not worked. He rejected all money and land grubbers out of hand. This ruled out the majority of his neighbors. Men of sufficiently ethical bent were either voting abolitionists and he was opposed to voting, or Garrisonian pacifists, love-alls, whose tendency to "cuddle up and lie spoon fashion with you" outraged him. He liked people who kept their distance and never called him "Henry."

Even casual, harmless conversation, little human byplay, annoyed him. "I would fain walk on the deep waters, but my companions will only walk on shallows and puddles." His friendship with Emerson was turning sour; in his *Journal* he speaks of him with hate. And above all he was stricken with that Timonism that Melville speaks of in *Pierre:* that black despair and hopelessness that comes to a serious writer when a book he *knows* is the best work he will ever be able to perform, falls flat and becomes, in a month or so, stale and unprofitable. He had written two fine books, *A Week* and *Walden.* Both were failures in a contemporary sense. Writing was his work and he wanted rewards for it, all across the board, and it is dehumanizing a writer to say that he does not, or is "above this."

He was keeping on with his journals, doggedly, joylessly. He plowed, sowed and reaped the Concord soil, season after season, casting up, year after year, the same rocks, sods and miniature life, while its fecundity, and his, drained away under the pitiless sun of reality. Like Pierre, perhaps, "at last the idea obtruded, that the wiser and profounder he would grow, the more and more he lessened his chances for bread; that could he now hurl his deep book out of the window, and fall on some shallow nothing of a novel . . . then he could reasonably hope for appreciation and cash."

The few patches of light and heat in these later journals are reflected from his awareness that the Abolitionist Revolution was drawing to its breaking point. It only needed some form of human embodiment; some indestructible man performing irrevocable deeds to make it wholly visible. In these years, or more precisely, in this year of 1857, Thoreau stood, as all revolutionaries do, in that awful limbo between moral suasion and the expressed will of the majority, waiting for someone to be "all transcendental" and supersede the common morality then prevailing: to commit some irrevocable revolutionary act. In short, to embody revolutionary morality.

Shortly after he had received Cholmondeley's letter, a man he could hold up to the light like an oak leaf, and study the transparency and wholeness of his form and function, stepped off the Boston train. It was John Brown, who in Kansas, at Pottawatomie, Black Jack and Osawatomie, had created at last for Abolitionism, a revolutionary presence. He had come East during a lull in the Kansas wars to raise money, guns and men. Brown carried a heavy carpet bag in his hand and in it was a long length of trace chain with the blood of his son rusting on it. John, his oldest son, had been dragged on bleeding feet for miles over a flinty, dried-up river bed in Kansas, by a U.S. Dragoon mounted on a horse ahead of him. His crime was that of accepting an elective office in the provisional and illegal Free State government of Kansas. Brown would throw this chain at the feet of a possible recruit, saying in his metalic voice, ringing with the demoniac clang of the single-minded prophet, "This treatment made my son a maniac, yes, a maniac."

This tall, gaunt, ceremonious man, with the curious mixture of Quaker and warrior in his dress, whose talk had the stately movement of Jeremy Taylor's prose, whose walk, like Mohammed's, was the hard, pounding stride of a man climbing an invisible hill, made his way to the office of the Kansas Aid Society on School Street. In charge there was Frank Sanborn, a young school teacher who lived in Concord, directly across from the Thoreaus' boarding house. "Thoreau," wrote Sanborn in his autobiography, "who had his own bone to pick with the civil government . . . was desirous of meeting Brown." Sanborn took the Captain to dine at the Thoreaus' table. After dinner, Sanborn left Thoreau and Brown discussing Kansas around the parlor fire.

So these two unique men, natural revolutionaries, faced one another that long winter afternoon while the red ashes slowly fell from the glowing logs. Both were surveyors trained in precise measurement, and Thoreau was happy to see that "he did not overstate anything, but spoke within bounds." The story of the encounter from the listener's point of view is well recorded in the *Journal* and the "Plea." Apparently most of the virtues Thoreau had been so desperately looking for in a friend, a cause, a society, rested in John Brown. We know the old Puritan would sooner say "God Damn" than address Thoreau as "Henry." We know of the depth and earnestness of the Captain's talk, mainly describing action that he had initiated and carried through. Thoreau must have looked in awe at the deep blue eyes, as cold as wintry mountain peaks shrouded in blue dusk, and yet with volcanoes burning underneath. He must have thought of what those eyes had looked upon that bloody night at Pottawatomie when the old man ordered the death of five men, put the tender flesh of five unresisting men to the edge of the sword. It was impossible not to think of Pottawatomie in Brown's presence. He never talked like a bloody-minded man but he told Thoreau, very markedly, "It is perfectly well understood that I would not be taken."

Yet there was no real communication between these men and

it is curious, perhaps tragic, that there was not. Captain Brown was not so transparent as he seemed to Emerson, who called him "the most transparent of men." Brown was capable of great revolutionary duplicity. He had come to Boston ostensibly to get supplies for the Free State cause in Kansas; actually it was to get control of two hundred Sharps' rifles owned by the Massachusetts Kansas Committee and stored at this time in Tabor, Iowa, to make a direct assault on what Thoreau called "The obscene temple of slavery." In his private judgement he had as much contempt for the fumbling of liberal Northern politicians in their struggle to make Kansas a free state as Thoreau did. But he covered this expediently, while acquiring the money, guns and men he needed for the act which had been the purpose of his life.

Thoreau himself felt, and later recorded, this lack of communication. He had a very curious juxtaposition in his *Journal* for October, 1859. "I subscribed a trifle when he was here three years ago; I had such confidence in the man,—that he would do right,— but it would seem that he had not confidence enough in me, nor in anybody else I know, to communicate his plans to us. . . . I do not wish to kill or be killed, but I can foresee circumstances in which both of these things would by me be unavoidable. In extremities I could even be killed."

Thoreau was wrong in one respect: Brown had confided his ultimate plan to four men that Thoreau knew intimately and two others that he knew casually. The Transcendentalists with whom Brown shared his revolutionary commitment had two attitudes that could bind them to a common cause with him. First of all they believed that the Constitution was anti-slavery in its intent. They felt that the South had usurped power to support its slave system and that the Jeffersonian doctrine that there were "sacred and sovereign rights reserved in the hands of the people, and judged by the Constitution (of England) unsafe to be delegated to any other judicature," gave them the right of a people's revolution against chattel slavery.

In the second place, they had divested themselves of that sterile individualism which still had Thoreau in its coils. They had joined the society that Thoreau's inner consciousness was demanding: a revolutionary society, built up out of the experience process by which an individual, acting under ethical compulsion, withdraws from the mass society around him, and after an existential pause, becomes fused in a common cause to transform the rejected society. This fusion, to a real revolutionary, is irrevocable, and to the death. The morality of the prevailing society becomes obsolete, and a new revolutionary morality takes over. This is a step some Transcendentalists found very easy to take. It is highly compatible with the Emersonian dictum that man himself is the lawgiver.

No one can deny that John Brown was aware of these fine distinctions and preconditions, after reading the letter with which he recruited Frank Sanborn to his side. "My dear Friend,—Mr. Morton has taken the liberty of saying to me that you felt half inclined to make a common cause with me. I greatly rejoice in this: for I believe when you come to look at the ample field I labor in, and the rich harvest which not only this entire country but the whole world during the present and future generations may reap from its successful cultivation, you will feel that you are entirely out of your element until you find that you are in it, an entire unit. . . . God has honored but comparatively a very small part of mankind with any possible chance for such mighty and soul satisfying rewards. . . . I expect nothing but to 'endure hardness'; but I expect to effect a mighty conquest, even though it be like the last victory of Samson. I felt for a number of years, in earlier life, a steady, strong desire to die; but since I saw any prospect of becoming a 'reaper' in the great harvest, I have not only felt quite willing to live, but have enjoyed life much; and am now rather anxious to live for a few years more."

With a similar appeal, the very essence of revolutionary renewal, Brown recruited Thomas Wentworth Higginson, Edwin Morton, and Theodore Parker. None of them ever mentioned it to Thoreau, although Sanborn later became Thoreau's biographer, saw him, almost daily, for years, and although carped at by many academics for his lapses in scholarly disciplines, knew the *man* rather than his literary corpus, much better than his critics are willing to admit.

Edwin Morton had been at Brook Farm as a lad. Like the others, he was a practicing Transcendentalist. He had the greatest admiration for Thoreau and his writings, and was as familiar with them as anyone in the country. While at Harvard he had written a review of *Walden* and *A Week* so laudatory that Thoreau made a special trip to his dormitory to present him with a copy of *A Week*. In one of Cholmondeley's last letters he sends regards to Morton through Thoreau, feeling that Morton was truly of Thoreau's intimate circle.

Thomas Wentworth Higginson, one of the most voluminous writers and chroniclers of this period, salted almost every one of his works with references to his intimacy with Thoreau. He had married Mary Channing, the sister of Thoreau's often constant companion, Ellery Channing. He also knew Thoreau through Harrison Blake, Thoreau's Worcester friend. Thoreau was a little too hard pan for Higginson, who was the dandy of the movement; he liked to live off the top and be around where the action was. However, he did respect Thoreau's political judgement and in his *Cheerful Yesterdays* he wrote, "During this time . . . my alienation from the established order was almost as great as that of Thoreau's." As for Theodore Parker, the great prophet of Transcendentalism, and a man completely organized for use, he was not intimate with Thoreau, but if he had thought he would be at all usable, he would have recruited him forthwith.

Why then, was it they, and not Thoreau, that the great Captain of Liberty picked for his little army? Why was Thoreau, in effect, blackballed from a society which may have redeemed him from long years of melancholy and despair . . . years of which he recorded, "My life is like a stream that is suddenly dammed and has no outlet: but it rises higher up the hills that shut it in, and will become a deep and silent lake." It was a *society* Thoreau needed; not individual friends. There are few pages in literature more agonizing to read than those in which Thoreau records his broken friendships:

And now another friendship is ended.
I do not know what has made my friend doubt me,
But I know in love there is no mistake
and that every estrangement is well founded. . . .

I know of no aeons, or periods, no life or death
but these meetings and separations. . . .

I have not yet known friendship to cease, I think.
I feel I have experienced its decaying.
Morning, noon and night
I suffer a physical pain, an aching of the breast
which unfits me for my task. . . .

A man cannot be said to succeed in this life
who does not satisfy one friend. . . .

What if we feel a yearning to which no breast answers?
I walk alone.
My heart is full, feelings impede the current of my thoughts.
I knock on the earth for my friend.
I expect to meet him at every turn, but no friend appears,
and perhaps none is dreaming of me.
I am tired of frivolous society in which silence
is forever the most natural and the best manners.
I would fain walk on the deep waters,
but my companions will only walk on shallows and puddles.

This is the dark, sick side of Thoreau's individualism, or isolation, or alienation. It explodes distantly, like some deep fissure in the earth's bed rock, disuniting and leaving forever flawed the wholeness of the terrain above. There were no heaps of brilliant fragments in the last journals to be fused into mosaics as clear and brilliant and indestructible as meteorites for another *Week* or *Walden.* But then came the great drama at Harper's Ferry and two fine fragments left by the visits of John Brown to his fireside became fabricated in the fiery furnace of the day and hour and gave Thoreau a wonderful wholeness again.

He had no time to string together, with a jeweler's touch, a glittering continuity of sentences seen glowing in the density of his minutiae like crystals in a cave. This was no *Walden,* conceived with such broad margins it could take eight years to shape it right. He had to forge this between the hammer and the anvil of desperate hours of chaos and confusion in which everything he had thought and known about John Brown was contradicted and denied in the public press and in the opinions it brought forth ... desperate hours, even minutes, where a good man's life and immortality were being pounded into a flat oblivion. "I think we should express ourselves at once, while Brown is alive. The sooner the better." He wrote this in a letter to Harrison Blake, asking for a meeting in Worcester where he could speak on The Character of Captain Brown, Now in the Clutches of the Slaveholder. He took eleven days to write his Plea for John Brown. In the first three pages of the address he used material from eleven different pages of his *Journal.*

The most significant element of his transference of his thoughts and words from private to public utterance came in the way he altered the impersonal character of the journal entries. Where he had written *I understand that* ... , he now said, *I heard him say that.* Or where it read in the *Journal, I have been told he made such a remark as this* ... from the platform he puts it bluntly .... *He said!* He was my friend, Thoreau was saying, proudly, and he may have told me more, trusted me with more, than the government can ever prove.

In spite of this bold, and politically dangerous identification and commitment, his reputation as a "loner," so individualistic he could never *act* in a common cause with anyone, dogged him to the end and kept him out of another society, formed to rescue John Brown from the clutches of the slaveholder. Amos Bronson Alcott, Thoreau's friend and neighbor, was proposing to a few companions that "There should be enough of courage and intrepidity,—in Massachusetts men,—to steal South, since they cannot march openly, rescue him from the slaveholders, the State and United States courts, and save him for the impending crisis. Captain Higginson would be good for the leadership, and No. 64 will be ready to march with the rest." No. 64 was Alcott himself. Thoreau was never asked and Alcott's journal, from which the prior quotes were taken, says indirectly why, a few days later. "It is well that they met [Brown and Thoreau], and Thoreau saw

what he sets forth as no one else can . . . Brown taking more to
the human side and driving straight at institutions, while Thoreau
contents himself with railing at and leaving them otherwise alone."

Alcott should have known from Thoreau's speech that he was
changing: that he was counting numbers at last, first empathizing
with the group. . . . "When I think of him and his six sons, and
his son-in-law, not to enumerate the others, enlisted for this
fight, proceeding coolly, reverently, humanely to work, for months
if not years, sleeping and waking upon it, summering and winter-
ing the thought, without expecting any reward but a good conscience, while almost all America stood ranked on the other side,
—I say again it affects me as a sublime spectacle. . . . These men, in
teaching us how to die, have at the same time taught us how to
live. . . ."

And then reaching hopefully for the masses, the millions: "The
newspapers seem to ignore, or perhaps are ignorant of the fact,
that there are at least as many as two or three individuals to a
town throughout the North who think as much as the present
speaker does about him and his enterprise. I do not hesitate to
say that they are an important and growing party. We aspire to
be something more than stupid and timid chattels, pretending to
read history and our Bibles, but desecrating every house and
every day we breathe in. Perhaps anxious politicians may prove
that only seventeen white men and five negroes were concerned
in the late enterprise; but their very anxiety to prove this might
suggest to themselves that all is not told. Why do they still dodge
the truth? They are so anxious because of a dim consciousness of
the fact, which they do not distinctly face, that at least a million
of the free inhabitants of the United States would have rejoiced
if it had succeeded."

There is still individualism there too, but it is no longer per-
meated with solipsism. It is the revolutionary individualism of
man *"coming out* from evil." "Any man knows when he is justified,
and all the wits in the world cannot enlighten him on that point.
The murderer always knows that he is justly punished; but when
a government takes the life of a man without the consent of his
conscience, it is an audacious government, and is taking a step
toward its own dissolution. Is it not possible that an individual
may be right and a government wrong? Are laws to be enforced
simply because they were made? or declared by any number of
men to be good, if they are *not* good? Is there any necessity for a
man's being a tool to perform a deed of which his better nature
disapproves? Is it the intention of law-makers that *good* men shall
be hung ever? . . . What right have *you* to enter into a compact
with yourself that you *will* do thus and so, against the light within
you? Is it for *you* to *make up* your mind,—to form any resolution

whatever,—and not accept the convictions that are forced on you, and which ever pass your understanding? . . . I plead not for his life but for his character, his immortal life, so it becomes your cause wholly and not his in the least."

Thus, with consummate brilliance, Thoreau sets up the push and pull of the dialogue between the findings and stirrings of the individual conscience and the mass action necessary to carry these findings to their resolution. The shy, woodsy little man who in 1855 told someone that he "suspected any enterprise in which two were engaged together," took on the sole sponsorship, and for a time, the total public defense of twelve traitors caught red-handed. The men Brown had chosen to help him, with the exception of Higginson, had vanished. Gerrit Smith went into an insane asylum. Sanborn and Doctor Howe went to Canada. Parker was already dying in Italy. Edwin Morton went so fast and so far that he was scoffingly referred to as "The wicked flea whom no man pursueth."

And so the stone the builder rejected became the foundation of all who have faith in him . . . and who believe today that he is still the greatest prophet in this accursed racist country where the black man still has no rights that the white man has to respect. The great abolitionists other than Brown have been downgraded for so many years now that they are practically exorcised from the American consciousness. Only Henry Thoreau has remained indestructible, escaped planned oblivion, and that only because of his consummate art. And all who pick up, or are taught *Walden* and *A Week* and are drawn by their magic into the totality of their author's work, come at last to his great plea for a still despised and defamed man who for fifty-six powder-blackened hours, amidst the bloody agonies of his dying comrades and his dying sons, was the conscience of the world.

In his lens-clear view of John Brown, Thoreau came finally to realize that there is an exalted form of individualism which merges into universality and becomes one with it. He expressed this best at the service held for Brown on the day of his hanging. "So universal and widely related is any transcendent moral greatness, and so nearly identical with greatness everywhere and in every age,— as a pyramid contracts the nearer you approach its apex,—that when I now look over my commonplace book of poetry, I find the best of it is oftenest applicable, in part, or wholly, to the case of Captain Brown." The key word here is pyramid, for greatness in any individual can only come when he rises as a symbolic peak out of a broad base below him; when he is literally lifted and held on the broad shoulders of men and women, like-minded with himself, whose common, whose multiple aspirations he embodies in his own selfless, revolutionary presence.

## THOREAU AND JOHN BROWN

Henry Thoreau shouldered and put along with for the rest of his life, the full burden of his responsibility and affinity to John Brown's revolutionary morality; to the tragic waste, the straits, the conspiracy, the killing, the tenderness, love and sacrifice, the whole diapason of upheaval that lesser men find so abhorrent. He did not safely and sentimentally enthuse over the overthrow or the attempted overthrow of tyrannies distant in time or place while knuckling under to the petty tyranny, the censure and threat coming from the wooden-headed reactionaries all about him, from questioning inquisitors and the policeman's violence that backs them up. Revolutions are bloody awful, no one argues that, but things have to be twice that bloody awful to make them work. This was the way things were with John Brown and Henry Thoreau. Both were real men in a real world. You have to take them as that or leave them alone.

# THOREAU'S POLITICS OF THE UPRIGHT MAN

## RICHARD DRINNON

"IN IMAGINATION I HIE ME TO GREECE as to an enchanted ground," Thoreau declared in his *Journal* and then proved himself as good as his word in his lecture on "The Rights & Duties of the Individual in relation to Government." There was not a majoɪ figure in the classical background of anarchism on whom Thoreau did not draw upon in some way. Though he may have been unaware of Zeno's strictures against Plato's omnicompetent state, he assuredly honored the Stoic for his individualism, his use of paradox, perhaps his belief in transcendent universal laws, certainly his serenity—"play high, play low," Thoreau observed with delight, "rain, sleet, or snow—it's all the same with the Stoic." He read Ovid with pleasure, used a quotation from the *Metamorphoses* as an epigraph for his *Week on the Concord and Merrimack Rivers,* and must have been well aware of Ovid's nostalgia for a time when there was no state and "everyone of his own will kept faith and did the right." But he found the most dramatic presentation of libertarian views in the *Antigone* of Sophocles. In this great drama of rebellion the central conflict was between the spirited Antigone and her uncle Creon, a not unkind man who had just ascended the throne of Thebes. Corrupted a little already by his power, blinded more than a little by bureaucratic definitions of right and wrong, and advancing specious reasons of state as justification for his actions, Creon forbade the burial of the dead traitor Polynices. Driven by love for her slain brother and more by her awareness of the unambiguous commands of the gods to bury the dead, Antigone defied Creon's order. When she was brought before the king, she proudly avowed her defiance:

> For it was not Zeus who proclaimed these to me, nor
> Justice who dwells with the gods below; it was not they
> who established these laws among men. Nor did I think
> that your proclamations were so strong, as, being a mortal,
> to be able to transcend the unwritten and immovable laws
> of the gods. For not something now and yesterday, but
> forever these live, and no one knows from what time they
> appeared. I was not about to pay the penalty of violating
> these to the gods, fearing the presumption of any man.[1]

---

[1] Thoreau's sturdy prose translations in the *Week, Writings* (1906), I, 139-40, may be compared with Gilbert Murray's rhyming verse translation

In his lecture on the individual and the state, which became the essay printed first as "Resistance to Civil Government" and later under the famous title "Civil Disobedience," Thoreau echoed Antigone's magnificent lines in his admission that "it costs me less in every sense to incur the penalty of disobedience to the State than it would to obey" and in his declaration that "they only can force me who obey a higher law than I." Like Sophocles' heroine, Thoreau made quite clear his rejection of the Periclean argument of Creon that the highest responsibility of the individual must be to the state and his rejection of the later Platonic assumption of a pleasing harmony between the laws of man and the laws of the gods. The kernel of Thoreau's politics was his belief in a natural or higher law; for the formulation of his essay on this subject, his indebtedness to the Greek tragedian was considerable.

Yet no single work provided Thoreau with his key concept.[2] In his day the doctrine of a fundamental law still covered Massachusetts like a ground fog. It had survived the classical period, had become the eternal law of Aquinas, the anti-papal fundamental law of Wycliffe, and, through Calvin, Milton, and Locke, had flowed across the Atlantic to furnish the colonists with their indispensable "Word of God." The more secular emphasis of the eighteenth century on the "unalienable Rights" possessed by every individual in a state of nature made little difference in end result—

---

of *Antigone* (London: Allen & Unwin, 1941), 37-38. As Murray remarked in the introduction, Sophocles seemed to have created the ideal virgin martyr of Greek tragedy almost in spite of his intention; it is highly improbable that he set out to create an anarchist heroine. Yet she demonstrated unforgettably a specific instance of the possible gap between justice and state law and the final responsibility the individual owes to those laws which are above and beyond the Creons of this world. In this ultimate sense Antigone was an anarchist heroine—with reason Henry Nevinson pointed this out years ago in an essay on "An Anarchist Play," *Essays in Freedom* (London: Duckworth, 1911), 209-14.

[2] Thanks to the careful researches of Ethel Seybold, *Thoreau: The Quest and the Classics* (New Haven: Yale University Press, 1951), 16, 17, 24, 66, 75, we know that Thoreau read the *Antigone* at Harvard and probably twice thereafter, once at the time he was working up his lecture on the dangers of civil obedience and once in the 1850's. Unfortunately Miss Seybold overstates her case by making the *Antigone* "probably responsible for one whole section of Thoreau's thought and public expression. From it must have come his concept of the divine law as superior to the civil law, of human right as greater than legal right." I say "unfortunately," because her overstatement has allowed some students to dismiss her valid points with rather fatuous pronouncements that Thoreau was merely an "involuntary classicist," that he was a "romanticist" by nature—whatever all this means. That Thoreau could find plenty of "romance" in the revels of the great god Pan, the mysticism of Orpheus, and the naturalness of Homer seems clear to me. In any event, one major inspiration for "Civil Disobedience" was Sophocles' work, first presented about 441 B.C., well in advance of Étienne de Boétie's *Discourse sur la Servitude Voluntaire*, published in 1577 and suggested as the earliest important source by Edward L. Tinker, *New York Times Book Review*, 29 March 1942.

little difference at least in doctrine, for all along men had thought it natural for a higher law to be the basis for legislation. In nineteenth-century Massachusetts the existence of a fundamental, higher law was accepted by radicals such as Alcott and Garrison, by liberals such as William Ellery Channing, and by conservatives such as Justice Joseph Story. These older countrymen of Thoreau were joined by Emerson, whose essay on "Politics," published five years before "Civil Disobedience," had a more direct influence on the young rebel. To be sure, Emerson approached the crass Toryism of Chancellor Kent in discussing "higher law" by attaching it to the power of property. But Emerson was usually much better—at his worst he could sound like an early incarnation of Bruce Barton—than his lines on wealth and property would suggest; most of "Politics" was on the higher ground of a radical Jeffersonianism:

> Hence the less government we have the better—the fewer laws and the less confided power. The antidote to this abuse of formal government is the influence of private character, the growth of the Individual . . . the appearance of the wise man; of whom the existing government is, it must be owned, but a shabby imitation. . . . To educate the wise man the State exists, and with the appearance of the wise man the State expires. The appearance of character makes the State unnecessary. The wise man is the State.[3]

Emerson even averred that "good men must not obey the laws too well."

The similarity of Emerson's point of view and even his language to Thoreau's must be clear to anyone who has carefully read "Civil Disobedience." Living where he did when he did, Thoreau could hardly have escaped the doctrine of a higher law. It was hardly fortuitous that *all* the most notable American individualist anarchists—Josiah Warren, Ezra Heywood, William B. Greene, Joshua K. Ingalls, Stephen Pearl Andrews, Lysander Spooner, and Benjamin Tucker—came from Thoreau's home state of Massachusetts and were his contemporaries. Tying the development of American anarchism to native traditions and conditions, Tucker uttered only a little white exaggeration when he claimed that he and his fellow anarchists were "simply unterrified Jeffersonian democrats."[4]

---

[3] *The Complete Essays* (New York: Modern Library, 1940), 431.

[4] Quoted in Rudolf Rocker, *Pioneers of American Freedom* (Los Angeles: Rocker Publications Committee, 1949), 150. A more recent and helpful study of early American anarchism is James J. Martin, *Men against the State* (DeKalb, Illinois: Adrian Allen Associates, 1953). The native Ameri-

Thus the doctrine of higher law, as Benjamin Wright once re-marked, logically leads to philosophical anarchism. True, but this truth can be misleading without the warning note that the logic has to be followed out to the end. Half-way covenants can lead to something very different. John Cotton, for instance, believed in a higher law, yet came down on the side of authority and the Massa-chusetts establishment; Roger Williams believed no less in a higher law, yet came down on the side of freedom and the individual. Like all ideas, that of a higher law could become a weapon in the hands of groups and institutions. For Thomas Aquinas *lex aeterna* meant the supremacy of the church, for Thomas Hobbes the "Law of Nature" meant the supremacy of the state. For Jefferson and Paine, natural law meant revolution and the establishment of a counter state. But for Thoreau it meant no supremacy of church over state or vice versa, or of one state over another, or of one group over another. It meant rather the logical last step of *indi-vidual action*. Belief in higher law *plus* practice of individual direct action *equal* anarchism. "I must conclude that Conscience, if that be the name of it," wrote Thoreau in the *Week,* "was not given us for no purpose, or for a hindrance." From Antigone to Bronson Alcott, Thoreau, and Benjamin Tucker, the individuals who acted on the imperatives of their consciences, "cost what it may," were anarchists.[5]

2

So much for the main sources and the master pillars of Thor-eau's political position. I have argued that in those crucial matters in which expediency was not applicable, it added up to anarchism. But the question of whether this made him a workaday anarchist lands us in the middle of a tangle. Was Thoreau really an individ-

---

can anarchists shared with Thoreau yet another Yankee characteristic: they were all members of an entrepreneurial professional middle-class which was integral to a relatively simple economy based on farming and trade. Not unnaturally they tended to assume that the interests of all would be best promoted if the individual were left absolutely free to pursue his self-in-terest. That is to say, just as they developed higher law doctrine to its logical conclusion, so did they take laissez faire theory beyond the liberals to advo-cate a marketplace literally without political controls. Fortunately Thoreau did not join these anarchists in their preoccupation with currency manipula-tion, free banking, economic competition. Aside from being more interesting, the trail Thoreau cut for himself promised to lead somewhere.

[5] In 1875 Tucker followed Thoreau's example and refused to pay the poll tax of the town of Princeton, Massachusetts; he was imprisoned in Worcester a short while for his refusal—see Martin, *Men against the State,* pp. 203-04. It had almost become a habit in the area. Three years before Thoreau spent his night in jail, Alcott was arrested for not paying his poll tax. Thoreau was probably influenced by his example and by the civil disobedience agita-tion of William Lloyd Garrison and his followers—see Wendell Glick, " 'Civil Disobedience': Thoreau's Attack upon Relativism," *Western Hu-manities Review,* VII (Winter 1952-53), 35-42.

ualist, an anarchist, or both, or neither? Emma Goldman defined anarchism as "the philosophy of a new social order based on liberty unrestricted by man-made law" and once spent an evening in Concord vainly trying to persuade Franklin Sanborn that under this definition Thoreau was an anarchist. Joseph Wood Krutch doubts that Thoreau felt a direct responsibility for any social order, old or new, and stresses his "defiant individualism."[6] Sherman Paul, on the other hand laments that "one of the most persistent errors concerning Thoreau that has never been sufficiently dispelled is that Thoreau was an anarchical individualist."[7] Still, "Thoreau was not an anarchist but an individualist," argues John Haynes Holmes.[8] The tangle becomes impassable with Paul's additional observation that Thoreau "was not objecting to government but to what we now call the State."

There are two main reasons for this muddle. Thoreau was himself partially responsible. His sly satire, his liking for wide margins for his writing, and his fondness for paradox provided ammunition for widely divergent interpretations of "Civil Disobedience." Thus, governments being but expedients, he looks forward to a day when men will be prepared for the motto: "That government is best which governs not at all." The reader proceeds through some lines highly critical of the American government, only to be brought up sharp, in the third paragraph, by the sweet reasonableness of the author: "But, to speak practically and as a citizen, unlike those who call themselves no-government men, I ask for, not at once no government, but *at once* a better government." Those who discount Thoreau's radicalism snap up this sentence which seems clear on the face of it: Do not think me an extremist like the Garrisonians and anarchists, he seems to be saying, but think of me as one who moderately desires a better government now. But is this all he wants? Might he not favor, *a little later,* no government? Shattered by this doubt, the reader is thrown forward into another bitter attack on the American government and on the generic state. It becomes increasingly clear that critics who have tried to put together a governmentalist from Thoreau's writings on politics have humorlessly missed the point. He does indeed say that he will take what he can get from the state, but he also twits himself a little for inconsistency: "In fact, I quietly declare war with the State, after my fashion, though I will still make what use and get what advantage of her I can, as is usual in such cases."

[6] Krutch, *Henry David Thoreau* (New York: William Sloane, 1948), 133-35.

[7] Paul, *The Shores of America: Thoreau's Inward Exploration* (Urbana: University of Illinois Press, 1958), 75-80, 377. Paul emphasizes Thoreau's willingness to have "governmental interference for the general welfare."

[8] Holmes, "Thoreau's 'Civil Disobedience,'" *Christian Century*, LXVI (January-June 1949), 787-89.

Henry David Thoreau, by Jo DAVIDSON · 1945 · detail from bronze model
*courtesy of the Estate of Jo Davidson · photo by Gottscho-Schleisner, N.Y.C.*

Henry David Thoreau, by MALVINA HOFFMAN · 1962 · bronze
*The Hall of Fame for Great Americans at New York University*

Compare Thoreau's wry position here with that of Alex Comfort, the English anarchist, written a hundred years later: "We do not refuse to drive on the left hand side of the road or to subscribe to national health insurance. The sphere of our disobedience is limited to the sphere in which society exceeds its powers and its usefulness. . . ."[9] But let us back up a bit. What was the nature of the "better government" he wanted at once? Obviously it was one that would stay strictly in its place and ungrow—progressively cease to exist. What was the "best government" he could imagine? He has already told us and the essay as a whole supports his declaration: a government "which governs not at all."

But the main obstacle to any clear cut identification of Thoreau's politics has been the uncertain shifting borders of anarchism, liberalism, and socialism in the nineteenth century and after. No series of definitions has succeeded in decisively marking out their frontiers. Stephen Pearl Andrews, for instance, the erudite contemporary of Thoreau, conceived of himself as at one and the same time a believer in the socialism of Charles Fourier and the anarchism of Josiah Warren. The intermingling of socialism and anarchism is further illustrated by Mikhail Bakunin, the founder of communist anarchism, who thought of himself as a socialist and fought Marx for the control of the First International. Even Marx has been called an ultimate anarchist, in the sense that he presumably favored anarchism after the state withered away. But perhaps the closest analogue to Thoreau was William Morris. Working closely with Peter Kropotkin for a number of years, Morris rejected the parliamentarians and joined forces with the libertarians in the Socialist League of the 1880's—the League was eventually taken over completely by anarchists!—and wrote *News from Nowhere* which was anarchist in tone and sentiment. Yet his explanation of why he refused to call himself an anarchist was obviously confused and showed that he was rejecting individualist anarchism and not Kropotkin's communist anarchism.[10]

A somewhat comparable confusion mars a recent attempt to analyze Thoreau's position. He was not "an anarchical individualist," argues Paul, because he went to Walden not "for himself alone but to serve mankind." It would be easy to quote passages from *Walden* which seem to call this contention into question. One ex-

---

[9] Quoted by Nicolas Walter, "Disobedience and the New Pacifism," *Anarchy*, No. 14 (April 1962), 113. It is worth noting that Walter thinks "Thoreau wasn't an anarchist," though he believes that "the implications of his action and his essay are purely anarchist. . . ." I am sure that Thoreau would have chuckled or perhaps laughed in his full free way had he known this question would still be debated a hundred years after his death.

[10] George Woodcock and Ivan Avakumovic, *The Anarchist Prince* (London: T. V. Boardman, 1950), 216-19. Thoreau's great influence on the English left dates back to this period when many were filled with idealism and with admiration for the "sublime doctrine" of anarchism.

ample: "What good I do, in the common sense of that word, must be aside from my main path, and for the most part wholly unintended." Another: "While my townsmen and women are devoted in so many ways to the good of their fellows, I trust that one at least may be spared to other and less humane pursuits."[11] Yet this would be to read Thoreau literally. Unquestionably, as he informed us in "Civil Disobedience," he was "as desirous of being a good neighbor as I am of being a bad subject." The distinction was crucial. Though he served the state by declaring war on it, in his own way, he served society for a lifetime by trying to understand and explain Concord to itself. The manageable unit of society— unlike the vast abstraction in Washington or even Boston—was drawn to the human scale of Concord and other villages. If men lived simply and as neighbors, informal patterns of voluntary agreement would be established, there would be no need for police and military protection, since "thieving and robbery would be unknown,"[12] and there would be freedom and leisure to turn to the things that matter. Thoreau's community consciousness was the essential, dialectical *other* of his individuality. Consider the following from *Walden:*

> It is time that villages were universities, and their elder inhabitants the fellows of universities, with leisure . . . to pursue liberal studies the rest of their lives. Shall the world be confined to one Paris or one Oxford forever? Cannot students be boarded here and get a liberal education under the skies of Concord? . . . Why should our life be in any respect provincial? If we will read newspapers, why not skip the gossip of Boston and take the best newspaper in the world at once. . . . As the nobleman of cultivated taste surrounds himself with whatever conduces to his culture—genius—learning—wit—books—paintings— statuary—music—philosophical instruments and the like; so let the village do. . . . To act collectively is according to the spirit of our institutions. . . . Instead of noblemen, let us have noble villages of men.[13]

---

[11] Since I have marked up my copy of *Walden* (New York: Modern Library, 1937), all my citations will be to this edition rather than to the appropriate Walden volume (II) of his *Works*. Here the quotations are from pp. 65, 66.

[12] *Walden*, 156.

[13] *Walden*, 98-100. By all means see Lewis Mumford's fine discussion of Thoreau in his chapter on "Renewal of the Landscape," in *The Brown Decades* (New York: Dover Publications, 1955), 64-72. Mumford credits Thoreau with the achievement of helping "to acclimate the mind of highly sensitive and civilized men to the natural possibilities of the environment" and gives him a major place in the history of regional planning in America. The influence of Thoreau on Paul Goodman, who describes himself as a "community anarchist," is apparent to anyone who has read his and his

One nobleman who also agitated for noble villages was the anarchist Kropotkin. He could have agreed completely with Thoreau's preoccupation with his locality and his readiness to act collectively "in the spirit of our institutions." In *Mutual Aid* (1902), Kropotkin celebrated the vital growth of society in the ancient Greek and medieval cities; he sadly outlined the consequences of the rise of centralization when the state "took possession, in the interest of minorities, of all the judicial, economical, and administrative functions which the village community already had exercised in the interest of all." Like Thoreau, Kropotkin advocated that the community's power be restored and that local individuality and creativity be left free to develop. The closeness of their views —though Kropotkin must have thought Thoreau too much an individualist like Ibsen!—points up the mistake of Sherman Paul and others in equating the "anti-social" with the "anarchical." Society and the state, as Thoreau and Kropotkin were very much aware, should not be confused or identified.

The definition of Emma Goldman quoted above will have to do for our purposes, then, though we must keep in mind its approximate nature and the greased-pole slipperiness of the political theory from which Thoreau's views are so often confidently said to have differed. Under this definition Thoreau was always an anarchist in matters of conscience, an ultimate anarchist for a time "when men are prepared for it," and in the meanwhile an anarchical decentralist. But enough of this attempt to stuff the poet and mystic in one political slot. Actually Thoreau's writings may yet help to explode all our conventional political categories.

### 3

"We scarcely know whether to call him the last of an older race of men, or the first of one that is to come," admitted an English critic in *The Times Literary Supplement* for 12 July, 1917. "He had the toughness, the stoicism, the unspoilt senses of an Indian, combined with the self-consciousness, the exacting discontent, the susceptibility of the most modern. At times he seems to reach beyond our human powers in what he perceives upon the horizon of humanity." With remarkable insight, the writer had perceived Thoreau's perplexing doubleness and had even touched the edge of his higher, profoundly exciting unity.

Of Thoreau's "unspoilt senses of an Indian" and his passion for the primitive there can be no question. "There is in my nature, methinks," he declared in the *Week,* "a singular yearning toward all wildness." To the end he was convinced that "life consists with

---

brother Percival's *Communitas* (Chicago: University of Chicago Press, 1947).

wildness." But this conviction did not rest on a sentimental-romantic view of our "rude forefathers." The crude relics of the North American tribes, their improvident carelessness even in the woods, and their "coarse and imperfect use" of nature repelled him. His unpleasant experience of a moose-hunt in Maine led to the reflection: "No wonder that their race is so soon exterminated. I already, and for weeks afterwards, felt my nature the coarser for this part of my woodland experience, and was reminded that our life should be lived as tenderly and daintily as one would pluck a flower."[14] Yet Thoreau never gave up his conviction that, standing so close, Indians had a particularly intimate and vital relationship with nature. "We talk of civilizing the Indian," he wrote in the *Week,* "but that is not the name for his improvement. By the wary independence and aloofness of his dim forest life he preserves his intercourse with his native gods, and is admitted from time to time to a rare and peculiar society with nature. He has glances of starry recognition to which our saloons are strangers."

By way of contrast, "the white man comes, pale as the dawn, with a load of thought, with a slumbering intelligence as a fire raked up, knowing well what he knows, not guessing but calculating; strong in community, yielding obedience to authority; of experienced race; of wonderful, wonderful common sense; dull but capable, slow but persevering, severe but just, of little humor but genuine; a laboring man, despising game and sport; building a house that endures, a framed house. He buys the Indian's moccasins and baskets, then buys his hunting-grounds, and at length forgets where he is buried and plows up his bones."[15] In this list of the bourgeois virtues, the keen, far-reaching social criticism of "Life Without Principle"—first entitled "Higher Law"—and indeed of *Walden* itself is anticipated. Calculating for the main chance, this obedient white man had cut his way through thousands of Indians in order to rush to the gold diggings in California, "reflect the greatest disgrace on mankind," and "live by luck, and so get the means of commanding the labor of others less lucky, without contributing any value to society! And that is called enterprise! I know of no more startling development of the immortality of trade. . . . The hog that gets his living by rooting, stirring up the soil so, would be ashamed of such company."[16] In this powerful essay on "Life Without Principle," he concluded that "there is nothing, not even crime, more opposed to poetry, to philosophy, ay, to life itself, than this incessant business." An economist of importance, as the first chapter of *Walden* may yet prove to a

---

[14] Quoted in Albert Keiser, *The Indian in American Literature* (New York: Oxford University Press, 1933), 227.

[15] *Works,* I, 52-53; see also 55.

[16] "Life without Principle," in *Walden,* 717.

skeptical world, Thoreau saw clearly that the accumulation of wealth really leads to the cheapening of life, to the substitution for man of the less-than-hog-like creature who calculates and lays up money and even fails to root up the soil in the process. "What is called politics," he wrote in "Life Without Principle," "is comparatively something so superficial and unhuman, that practically I have never fairly recognized that it concerns me at all." The war against Mexico, the scramble for territory and power, and other debauches in nationalism were, he trusted, a different manifest destiny from his own. In his letter to Parker Pillsbury on the eve of the fighting at Fort Sumter, he reported that he did "not so much regret the present condition of things in this country (provided I regret it at all) as I do that I ever heard of it. I know one or 2 who have this year, for the first time, read a president's message; but they do not see that this implies a fall in themselves, rather than a rise in the president. Blessed were the days before you read a president's message. Blessed are the young for they do not read the president's message."[17] Yet, despite all these devastating shafts aimed at the institutions reared up by the "pale as dawn" white man, Thoreau honored learning as much or more than any man in America. Far from advocating a return to some preliterate bliss, he advocated, in his chapter on "Reading" in *Walden,* a study of "the oldest and the best" books, whose "authors are a natural and irresistible aristocracy in every society, and, more than kings or emperors, exert an influence on mankind."

Thus Thoreau's doubleness, of which he was well aware: "I find an instinct in me conducting to a mystic spiritual life, and also another to a primitive savage life." It was one of his great achievements to go beyond the polarities of "Civilization and Barbarism" —alternatively attractive poles which drew most of Thoreau's contemporaries helplessly back and forth like metal particles—to come close to a creative fusion: "We go eastward to realize history and study the works of art and literature, retracing the steps of the race," he wrote in the serene summary of his walks. "We go westward as into the future, with a spirit of enterprise and adventure." Thoreau wanted the best for his countrymen from both nature and civilization, past and present. He perceived clearly the meaning of America. It was an opportunity for new beginnings: "The Atlantic is a Lethean stream, in our passage over which we have had an opportunity to forget the Old World and its institutions. If we do not succeed this time, there is perhaps one more chance for the race left before it arrives on the banks of the Styx; and that is

---

[17] His reference to "manifest destiny" appeared in his letter to H. G. O. Blake, 27 February, 1853; his letter to Pillsbury was dated 10 April, 1861— *The Correspondence of Henry David Thoreau,* eds. Walter Harding and Carl Bode (New York: New York University Press, 1958), 296, 611.

in the Lethe of the Pacific, which is three times as wide." Had he lived with unflagging powers for another decade or so, he might have used his laboriously accumulated notebooks of "Extracts relating to the Indians" to show why the aborigines enjoyed "a rare and peculiar society with nature."[18] It is indisputable that his interest in classical mythology, ancient societies, and contemporary tribes was an anthropological concern for the enduring features of life in groups. His interest in savages was much like that of Claude Lévi-Strauss and might have been expressed in the latter's words: "The study of these savages does not reveal a Utopian state in Nature; nor does it make us aware of a perfect society hidden deep in the forests. It helps us to construct a theoretical model of society which corresponds to none that can be observed in reality, but will help us to disentangle 'what in the present nature of Man is original, and what is artificial.' "[19] Thoreau's theoretical model, which came from all his efforts to drive life into a corner and get its measurements, made it clear that the efforts of his neighbors to live for the superfluous made their lives superfluous. Through careful inspection of his model, he was able to see, years before Lenin, that at bottom the state is a club. To cooperate with it, especially in matters of importance, is to deny life, for the state, like a standing army, is organized power and at the disposal of hate. "You must get your living by loving," confidently declared this supposedly narrow village eccentric. Clearly, he aspired to create for his countrymen a "new heaven and a new earth," just as each of Greece's sons had done for her. The look of this new heaven is suggested by a passage in the *Week*. On Saturday, after he and John had made the long pull from Ball's Hill to Carlisle Bridge, they saw "men haying far off in the meadow, their heads waving like the grass which they cut. In the distance the wind seemed to bend all alike. As the night stole over, such a freshness was wafted across the meadow that every blade of cut grass seemed to teem with life."

To this feeling of the correspondence of man to nature, "so that

---

[18] Keiser, *The Indian in American Literature*, 217-18, "cannot but believe that cruel fate robbed the world of a great work dealing in a sanely realistic yet sympathetic . . . manner with the child of nature on the American continent. . . ." Perhaps, though it is possible that the Civil War might have undone Thoreau along with so many others. It should be noted that Thoreau shows, in many passages, an intuitive sense of the distinction, made by such modern students as Mircea Eliade, between cyclical archaic time and progressive, cumulative modern time. His works were organized around the former. Indeed the *Week* might be interpreted as an extended defense of Parmenides's thesis of the permanence of the universe against the Heraclitean progressivism of a nation of boosters (see esp. 54-56, 60, 128, 239, 347, 416). His constant return to the problem of time and its obvious importance for his understanding of man in nature invite a careful, systematic inquiry.

[19] Lévi-Strauss, "Tristes Tropiques," *Encounter*, XC (April 1961), 40.

he is at home in her," Thoreau added poetic intuitions of an individualism to come. With his common sense, he realized that the notorious common sense of his countrymen was insane. The important questions were buried under daily rounds of trivia. Living was constantly deferred. No joyful exuberance was allowed to slip by prudence. Thoreau could have joined William Blake in his belief that "Prudence is a rich, ugly old maid, courted by Incapacity." The incapacity was partly the result of a split between the head and the heart, thought and feeling, and the absurd belief that the intellect alone enables man to meet life. In his final summing up, in the essay "Walking," he warned that the most we can hope to achieve is "Sympathy with Intelligence . . . a discovery that there are more things in heaven and earth than are dreamed of in our philosophy." But his neighbors not only had an overfaith in abstract reasoning and in the general efficacy of the intellect; they also distrusted the body. William Blake could thrust through the prudishness of his time to rediscover the body; hemmed in by the moral sentimentalism of his family, by Emersonian etherealness, and his own confirmed virginity, Thoreau had more difficulty. His embarrassing admission—"what the essential difference between man and woman is, that they should be thus attracted to one another, no one has satisfactorily answered"—is indeed, as Krutch points out, "a real howler."[20] Nevertheless, he took a sensuous delight in his body, claiming in the *Week* that "we need pray for no higher heaven than the pure senses can furnish, a purely sensuous life. Our present senses are but rudiments of what they are destined to become." Here is a body mysticism which placed Thoreau in the tradition of Jacob Boehme and William Blake. It presupposed, Norman Brown observes, that "the consciousness strong enough to endure full life would be no longer Apollonian but Dionysian—consciousness which does not observe the limit, but overflows; consciousness which *does not negate any more.*"[21] Shocked by phallic forms in nature, the stiff-backed Thoreau yet remarked that he worshipped most constantly at the shrine of Pan —Pan, the upright man of the Arcadian fertility cult, famous for his Dionysiac revels with the mountain nymphs![22] The vision of individuals with spiritual development and the simple animal strength to affirm their bodies was one of the important contributions of this paradoxical celibate. It was a vision sensed and acted upon, in their own ways, by Isadora Duncan and Emma Goldman

[20] Krutch, *Thoreau*, 207.

[21] Brown, *Life against Death* (Middletown, Conn.: Wesleyan University Press, 1959), 308-11.

[22] *Works*, I, 65. I should not place any great reliance on this passage, which apparently was valued in part for its shock value, if it stood alone. It does not.

and Randolph Bourne and Frank Lloyd Wright. It exerts its appeal to the poetic libertarian strain in radicalism, to men as diverse as e. e. cummings, Karl Shapiro, Henry Miller, Paul Goodman, Kenneth Patchen, Herbert Read, the late Albert Camus and Nicolas Berdyaev. A recent, rather extravagant form is perhaps Allen Ginsberg's notion of "Socialist-Co-op Anarchism." In any form it is revolutionary.

"One thing about Thoreau keeps him very near to me," Walt Whitman remarked. "I refer to his lawlessness—his dissent—his going his absolute own road let hell blaze all it chooses."[23] Thousands of young people know exactly what Whitman meant. A few perhaps can see that Thoreau's death was his greatest achievement, for it showed that his philosophy had taught him how to die—and therefore how to live. Some can appreciate and understand his two years at Walden Pond. But many are ready, like the young Indian lawyer in South Africa in 1907, to be impressed that Thoreau "taught nothing he was not prepared to practice in himself."[24] Like Gandhi, they are ready to draw on Thoreau's "Civil Disobedience" for "a new way" of handling political conflict. Thoreau thereby made another major contribution to radical politics, for anarchism and socialism have traditionally been strong on ends and weak or worse on means. It is true that Thoreau was himself unclear about violence, as his splendid tribute to John Brown and his occasional callow observations on war show—"it is a pity," he wrote a correspondent in 1855, "that we seem to require a war from time to time to assure us that there is any manhood still left in man."[25] Yet he went farther than most in thinking his way through this problem. More importantly, like Antigone he left us the powerful, burning, irresistible appeal of his example. It is as timely as the banner "Unjust Law Exists" which marched beside Camus' "Neither Victims Nor Executioners" in the recent Washington youth demonstrations. It is as timely as Bertrand Russell's sit-down in Trafalgar Square. It may even help us survive the disease called modern history.

---

[23] Quoted by Walter Harding, *A Thoreau Handbook* (New York: New York University Press, 1959), 201.

[24] Quoted by George Hendrick, "The Influence of Thoreau's 'Civil Disobedience' on Gandhi's *Satyagraha*," *New England Quarterly*, XXIX (1956), 464.

[25] Letter to Thomas Cholmondeley, 7 February 1855—see *Correspondence of Thoreau*, 371.

# HENRY THOREAU ONCE MORE

## STANLEY EDGAR HYMAN

IN THESE PAGES, too, the *I*, or first person, will be retained. In 1946, in my twenty-seventh year, I published an essay called "Henry Thoreau in Our Time." With ironic suitability, it appeared in *The Atlantic Monthly*, a magazine to which Thoreau would not submit anything after its editor censored a "pantheistic" sentence. My essay, which ran to other heresies than pantheism, was an attempt to define a Thoreau who still spoke to our condition in 1946. I saw myself, with considerable presumption, as speaking for a young literary generation which had come through the strident politics of the 1930s, then the war, and now lived under a mushroom shadow.

I concluded that the essential Thoreau for our purposes was the *writer* who had made the diamond of "Civil Disobedience" out of the soft coal of his somewhat ludicrous night in jail. Thoreau's message, in brief, was that the writer's place is not on the picket line nor even on the Admirable Cause Committee, but at his desk, writing the truth as he sees it. My essay went into other matters: it discussed the ritual cycles that underlie *Walden*, and it turned a mild Freudian eye on some images, but its real point was to find or create a Thoreau relevant to myself and to anyone who might share my predicament.

In the years since, I have been faithful to that image—I am a member of no incorporated body but the American Numismatic Society and the human race—but recently I have begun to think that my Thoreau must be hopelessly outdated, that in a world of space travel and Freedom Riders there must be newer images of Thoreau. In quest of them I have read half a dozen recent books on the man, chosen at random, since I am no Thoreau scholar. I must report that I find no images of Thoreau more attractive than my own, and that some are considerably less attractive.

Henry Beetle Hough's *Thoreau of Walden: The Man and His Eventful Life* (1956), a popular biography, is the most inconsequential book of those I read, and its image most patently a travesty. Hough is the editor of a country weekly, the *Vineyard Gazette,* and the author of a number of benign books about small-town life. His Thoreau might be the folksy editor of the *Walden Gazette,* not the author of "Slavery in Massachusetts," who picked up newspapers and "heard the gurgling of the sewer through every column."

This Thoreau has been mightily tamed. His *Walden,* in Hough's eyes, is "a book as native as the huckleberry bushes," and if it has the bad taste to say that the farmer spends his lifetime digging his grave with a plow, Hough will repair things: "the farmer deserved credit for being a farmer." Discussing Thoreau's signing off from the Unitarian Church, Hough writes: "There were surely lively discussions of this affair at the Thoreau home, and it must have distressed the family to see Henry making himself conspicuous and to some people offensive through his studied nonconformity. Majority feeling in New England was always against 'scenes' and this was a 'scene' of a kind." Commenting on Samuel Hoar's paying the poll tax Alcott refused to pay, Hough writes, having it both ways: "Governments would suffer more for their sins if it were not for men like Squire Hoar, and so would idealists like Bronson Alcott."

The phrase that perhaps most clearly shows Hough's absolute inadequacy to his subject is a reference to "the Thoreau sort of people." Hough really is a terrible cornball. He writes of Thoreau's letter to Lidian Emerson: "The phrases of the heart were such as any woman might prize coming from any man who loved her much." Hough describes Thoreau's prose as "sentences bold and rhythmic like the tall, swaying limbs of great trees." His own prose dissolves everything it touches, and it can digest even cellulose.

Leo Stoller's *After Walden: Thoreau's Changing Views on Economic Man* (1957) is a 1956 doctoral dissertation at Columbia, and is thus the view of a younger generation than my own. Its thesis, which is presented eloquently and well, is that Thoreau lost his faith in natural goodness climbing Mt. Katahdin in 1846, and as a consequence turned "away from utopian social thought and toward a new synthesis." This involved in principle "the acceptance of industrial capitalism," to be reformed and ameliorated rather than abolished, and in practice a yielding "to expediency" by surveying woodlots and thus contributing to their destruction.

In Stoller's view, Thoreau found a "union of principle and expediency" in the idea of forest management, which combines profits with forest preservation, and this union typifies his later social thought. Thus Thoreau "began to accept the industrial mode of production, to separate his concept of simplicity from handicrafts and subsistence farming, and to sketch a framework by which simplicity might be combined with industrialism." The "politics complementary to his economics," Stoller believes, was the young Republican Party, which should have been Thoreau's party.

This is an interesting and challenging thesis, but several things must be said. First, that Stoller sometimes reads Thoreau very badly—I did not trust him after page 50, when he identified "the journal of no very wide circulation" in *Walden* as the *Dial*, when it is of course Thoreau's *Journal*. Second, Stoller has no appreciation of the nature and importance of symbolic action, and writes flatly of "the failure of the Walden experiment." Third, his thesis is a considerable oversimplification of a much more complex social attitude, and there is plenty of evidence to the contrary, some of which Stoller presents.

Commenting on a demand for town forest-wardens in the 1860 *Journal,* Stoller observes that it is inconsistent with "Civil Disobedience." As he notes elsewhere, there is a strand of "Civil Disobedience" with which it is not at all inconsistent, that strand saying: "I have never declined paying the highway tax, because I am as desirous of being a good neighbor as I am of being a bad subject." Stoller properly notes that in his last years Thoreau turned against the institution of private property itself. But Stoller's quotations make this seem earnest and theoretical, not, as it was, gleefully subversive. Thoreau wrote to Harrison Blake welcoming the panic of 1857, with its failures of businesses and banks: "The statement that ninety-six in a hundred doing such business surely break down is perhaps the sweetest fact that statistics have revealed,—exhilarating as the fragrance of sallows in spring." As for the Republican Party, Stoller should take another look at "A Plea for Captain John Brown."

*The Shores of America: Thoreau's Inward Exploration* (1958), by Sherman Paul, is an intellectual or spiritual biography; "a biography of a vocation," Paul says. As such, it studiously and lovingly gives us the least important and least engaging Thoreau, the introspective self-important pest, the naturalist pursuing his soul with a butterfly net. Paul restores the Thoreau his contemporaries saw: heavily Transcendental and Emersonian. In this view, living at Walden was "the richest fulfillment of his life," and *Walden,* written "in his years of decay," "was written to summon it [that ecstasy] again." Everything becomes spiritual allegory: "the pond was the real self and the shore the empirical self"; "the pond was the soul"; "his vital heat [was] his faith" and so on. As a failure of nerve on Katahdin is helpful to Stoller's view, so a severe breakdown in 1850 is useful to Paul. Through the Pond experience all was harmonious; afterwards "the remainder of his life had its own quiet desperation," with the "years of crisis" beginning in 1850. Yet as early as 1843, as Paul shows, Thoreau wrote that he was "a diseased bundle of nerves," and Paul himself calls the experience at the Pond "effective therapy."

Paul supplements his old-fashioned image of Thoreau with several more modish ones. Following Edward Dahlberg, he compares Thoreau repeatedly to Randolph Bourne; and following F. O. Matthiessen, he compares him to Hemingway, although chiefly in terms of "reportorial skill." Two other images are fresher. Thoreau was "what we would call today an inner-directed man," and he demonstrated what David Riesman calls "the nerve of failure." At the same time, he was an *angst*-ridden Existentialist, revealing in his *Journals* "the gathering despair of his life." (More properly, an *angst*-ridden Essentialist, since Paul quotes his statement in an early *Journal:* "What a man does, compared with what he is, is but a small part.") Paul's book is, in short, a masterly means to an unimproved end.

*Consciousness in Concord* (1958) is an edition of Thoreau's hitherto "Lost Journal" of 1840-1841, edited with an extensive commentary by Perry Miller. Miller is one of the few authors of books on Thoreau who neither worship him nor identify with him, and Miller's tart maliciousness is a relief after all the cloying sweetness. His editing of the *Journal* is exhaustive and resourceful: noting revisions, tracing passages into print, identifying, explaining, raising the right questions and providing many of the right answers. Miller's general line is that "the *Journal* is so thoroughly a literary exercise that I am wary of biographical interpretations," but that does not keep him from finding in it an "embarrassing revelation of Thoreau's primal urge to find a 'mother-substitute' in impersonal nature," or anything else, when he chooses. As a key to the life, Miller sees Thoreau as secretly wishing and courting failure. Although all the Transcendentalists devoted themselves to "perfecting devices for being let down by their friends," "with Thoreau a luxuriating in friendship and in its inadequacies becomes simply monstrous." Miller mocks Thoreau as "this home-centered youth," writing "strangulated pages" out of "a syndrome of sensibility."

Nor is Thoreau his only butt. With Miller "we measure the sublimity of Emerson's insensitivity"; we are introduced to William Ellery Channing as "the poet who exalted the Transcendental imperative into a long life of irresponsible whim"; Miller cuts a letter from Isaiah Williams with the explanation: "A little bit of his screaming will suffice." Miller's style is as lively as his opinions. He squeezes the juice out of metaphors, he peppers parentheses with exclamation points, his diction is classroom-breezy. At one point I found Miller's book moving, when he introduces a long footnote about Thoreau's love for music with the statement: "This is one of those passages in Thoreau that break your heart." I hadn't known that Miller cared, and I rejoice.

Walter Harding is our most tireless Thoreauvian, and his *A Thoreau Handbook* (1958) offers itself as "a guide through the welter of Thoreau scholarship." As such it is excellent, handling an enormous amount of material with discernment and fairness in 200-odd pages. In regularly pointing out work that still needs doing, Harding sets useful targets for future Thoreau scholarship, although his principal demand—"we do not yet have a really satisfactory biography"—is easier to announce than to gratify.

In his own criticism of Thoreau in the book, Harding tends to warm tints, although there are occasional Millerite judgments: *A Week on the Concord and Merrimack Rivers* contains "passages vapid enough to have been written by Bronson Alcott"; the essay on "Love" contains, "as Krutch suggests, 'a real howler' "; the essay on "Chastity and Sensuality" is, if possible, "even more vapid." Harding ventures a few general interpretations: that Thoreau was no Stoic, that he is "America's greatest nature writer." But most of the book's value, in accord with its intention, is as a guide to other people's work, and as a mine of information. I did not know, for example, that the nudists have adopted Thoreau as a founding father, or that Gene Tunney read Thoreau as he trained for Jack Dempsey, and announced: "the spirit of Thoreau lends its luminous wisdom to man and nature wherever they meet," or that Lin Yutang regarded Thoreau as "the most Chinese of all American authors." I feel the better for the knowledge.

The latest of these books, Mark Van Doren's *Henry David Thoreau: A Critical Study* (1961) is also the earliest of them. It is a photographic reprint of Van Doren's undergraduate honors thesis at the University of Illinois, first published in 1916. As a piece of work by an undergraduate it is brilliant, even staggering, in my opinion the best criticism that Van Doren ever wrote.

Done under the supervision of Stuart P. Sherman, a pupil of Irving Babbitt's, and much influenced by Paul Elmer More, whom it describes as "Thoreau's most discriminating critic," the book takes the stand that was later to be identified as the New Humanism. Thoreau, along with Emerson, is accused of plunging "into shoreless seas of intellectual and moral egotism," of being ridden by "the intellectual demon." Van Doren sees Thoreau as emotionally defective, constitutionally lacking "a living heart," consisting of "little else than intellect." (Van Doren mockingly quotes John Burroughs—"If Thoreau had made friends with a dog to share his bed and board in his retreat by Walden Pond, one would have had more faith in his sincerity"—but does not realize how close his charges are to Burroughs'.) In one of the most whopping misstatements ever made about Thoreau, Van Doren writes: "Certainly the troubles of mankind caused him no disturbance."

In respect to Thoreau's emotional defects, Van Doren is misled by Emerson's obtuse tribute: "He had no temptations to fight against—no appetites, no passions." At the same time, Van Doren sees through Emerson's Stoic Thoreau, replaces it with an "out-and-out Epicurean" Thoreau, and then explodes that in turn with a Diogenes-the-Cynic Thoreau. (At least Van Doren makes it obvious to us that our Concord pea is somewhat too protean to stay under any of the walnut shells of Greek philosophy.)

Despite all of this nervous categorizing, the young Van Doren finds some aspects of Thoreau enormously attractive to him. He pleads for discounting: "Thoreau's permanent, best qualities—his sly and edged excellence, his leavening power—come into fuller recognition as his less essential qualities are subtracted and retreat." He asks that Thoreau be not read literally, but taken "with the sufficient allowance of salt." "If read as scripture, as some of his friends read him," Van Doren explains, "or as madman, as Lowell read him, he will yield nothing."

Early in his book, Van Doren announces that "the personality of Thoreau has never been presented in full, mainly because it has been treated in no case by any one who was not interested in proving a point." But Van Doren is as tendentious as his predecessors, as we all are and must be. He wants the "good hater and refuser," the nay-sayer, and he wants him as an image for himself and his generation. "Thoreau will be found a very satisfactory spokesman," Van Doren proclaims, "for one who feels driven into a position somewhat analogous to his position in 1840." Van Doren calls up "his support when it is necessary that one be unreasonable." Thoreau, he concludes, is "valuable as a protestant, valuable as an antidotal flavor."

\*     \*     \*

Perhaps the new images of Thoreau by the young will come only when some of the recent and forthcoming *Walden* scholarship —including Shanley's study of the drafts (1957), Sherwin and Reynolds' *Word Index* (1960), and Harding's *Variorum* (1962) —has been digested. The only example of such an image in the books I read—Stoller's compromiser—may be what the new generation wants, but it seems to me much less nourishing than Van Doren's refuser in 1916.

Paul's stab at an Existentialist *angst*-ridden Thoreau may be only the first of many such moves. Perhaps Henry Miller's "cool" Thoreau in his preface to *Life Without Principle: Three Essays by Henry David Thoreau* (1946)—the Thoreau "who would not run around the corner to see the world blow up"—will yet have a progeny of Beat and offbeat Thoreaus. *Civil Disobedience* has been a handbook for the Freedom Riders, as for Gandhi before them, and Integrationist Thoreaus are probably on their way. (I can even see a possible Black Muslim Thoreau, taking as its text the sneering contrast in *Walden* between the fake white runaway slaves and the real black runaway slave.)

"There are probably words addressed to our condition exactly," Thoreau wrote in *Walden*. "I want something speaking in some measure to the condition of muskrats and skunk-cabbage as well as of men," he wrote in his *Journal* in 1850. The problem is, of course, knowing what our condition is. If we can discover it, and whether it is that of men or skunk-cabbages, we can find a Thoreau to speak to it. Perhaps the years since 1945 have been years of such demoralization and dazzlement that our condition escapes us. If we ever rediscover what we are, we can expect Henry Thoreau to have been one too a century before.

Until then we can ask a few simple things of books on Thoreau, or judge them by a few simple tests. One is that they allow him on occasion to have behaved badly. The obvious example is the lecture to John Field the bog hoer in *Walden*. Thoreau took shelter from the rain in Field's house and "tried to help him with my experience," advising him to give up tea, coffee, butter, milk, and meat; to build himself a "palace" like Thoreau's; and so forth. When Field properly ignored him, Thoreau concluded: "But alas! the culture of an Irishman is an enterprise to be undertaken with a sort of moral bog hoe." He ends the chapter: "Poor John Field! —I trust he does not read this, unless he will improve by it."

This is a Thoreau oblivious to his principles and contemptuous of another man's privacy in his ways; Thoreau being a bore and a prig. Had one of "the self-styled reformers, the greatest bores of all," come at Thoreau in his hut with a similarly patronizing uplift, Thoreau would have booted him out the door. Characteristically, Hough approves of the mission to John Field, Stoller objects to it for the wrong reasons (because Thoreau did not give him *practical* advice), and Harding ignores it but observes that in general Thoreau befriended Irish immigrants.

The second test for a book on Thoreau is that it recognize that he was primarily a writer, not a naturalist, reformer, or whatever. Here the recent authors seem finally to have gotten the point. For all the brilliance of his analysis, Van Doren could not see that primacy in 1916. He writes typically: "No other naturalist has been so malicious; no other transcendentalist has been so fastidious." But Stoller pays tribute to Thoreau's "greatness both as man and writer," and Paul announces: "If anything he was a writer."

One of the pleasures of reading books on Thoreau is that they quote lines one didn't know or had forgotten. Here are a few that delighted me: of Alcott, "the rats and mice make their nests in him"; in 1841, "I exult in stark inanity, leering on nature and the soul"; of November, "Now a man will eat his heart, if ever"; mysteriously, in the "lost" *Journal,* "Every maggot lives down town"; of clergymen, that they cannot butter their own bread yet "make dipped toast for all eternity"; of a man who wanted to get rich to have leisure for poetry, "He should have gone up to the garret at once." Yet, like any writer, Thoreau is sometimes awful. He becomes Thornton W. Burgess when he discovers a new species of fish and protests in his *Journal* that the importance of the discovery is not in the scientific gain, "but that I have a little fishy friend in the pond."

The last test I would recommend for works on Thoreau is that they stop telling us that he was a Transcendentalist and tell us instead how he transcended Transcendentalism. "In his writing and in his living," Van Doren notes, "his genius for the specific, his preoccupation with details, his love of facts, and his passion for real experience mark him off as distinctly as is possible from his transcendental brethren." Van Doren later adds Thoreau's handiness with tools and his humor. This needed saying in 1916, and it still needs saying. Every time I have gone back to him Thoreau has seemed less Emersonian, and perhaps someday he will not seem Emersonian at all.

Matthiessen's *American Renaissance* (1941), which is *still* our best account of Thoreau (as it is our best account of Melville and so many others), said accurately: "His vitality as a revolutionary is still unexhausted." A young scholar, Wendell Glick, wrote in an article in 1952: "Thoreau's chief purpose in 'Civil Disobedience' was to wean men away from their adherence to an insidious relativism and to persuade them to return again to the superior standard of absolute truth." Perhaps those statements combine to make the best image of Thoreau we can take into the future: a revolutionary of absolute truth.